CAN YOU BEAT CHURCHILL?

CAN YOU BEAT CHURCHILL?

Teaching History through Simulations

MICHAEL A. BARNHART

CORNELL UNIVERSITY PRESS
ITHACA AND LONDON

First published 2021 by Cornell University Press

Library of Congress Cataloging-in-Publication Data

Names: Barnhart, Michael A., 1951– author.
Title: Can you beat Churchill? : teaching history through simulations / Michael A. Barnhart.
Description: Ithaca : Cornell University Press, 2021. | Includes bibliographical references and index.
Identifiers: LCCN 2020039959 (print) | LCCN 2020039960 (ebook) | ISBN 9781501755644 (Hardcover) | ISBN 9781501758294 (Paperback) | ISBN 9781501755668 (PDF) | ISBN 9781501755651 (ePub)
Subjects: LCSH: Simulation games in education. | History—Study and teaching—Simulation methods.
Classification: LCC LB1029.S53 B37 2021 (print) | LCC LB1029.S53 (ebook) | DDC 371.39/7—dc23
LC record available at https://lccn.loc.gov/2020039959
LC ebook record available at https://lccn.loc.gov/2020039960

To my mother, Ann Harrison, and my wife, Janet

Contents

Acknowledgments

Teaching by simulation is inherently a collaborative work. My collaborators over the years would number in the thousands, but they fall into three primary groups that deserve mention here.

First in line would be the many undergraduates at Stony Brook University who participated in—really, created themselves—the various simulations I have overseen there, especially in my *Great Power Rivalries 1936–1947* simulation seminar. It is a measure of their enthusiasm and dedication that over forty of them would return to the university at a recent homecoming to participate in a rapid rendition of the Cuban Missile Crisis. One sim-alum Skyped in from Moscow. Obviously, we put him on the Soviet team.

Second come my colleagues at Stony Brook. An exceptionally congenial History Department afforded me the opportunity to try out my ideas, and exceptionally gracious colleagues quickly turned from skeptics to cheerleaders. I owe individual mention to Eric Zolov, who actually took the plunge himself and now uses simulations in his courses, and to Seth

Offenbach, now teaching at Bronx Community College. Sharing his experiences with his classroom simulations was of great help as I prepared this book.

Not least would be instructors at other institutions, especially those active in the Reacting to the Past project based at Barnard College, who use classroom simulations. The Reacting community is just that, and its resources have helped me immeasurably. I am especially grateful to two of its members, John Moser of Ashland University and Robert Goodrich at Northern Michigan University. John graciously allowed me to use materials from his masterly simulation on Japan, and I enjoyed our discussions of its various features and workings. Robert conducted a fascinating simulation of the last years of the Weimar Republic that I participated in at a recent Reacting conference. My experience was memorable. His experience in dealing with abhorrent words and ideas in the classroom was invaluable.

Emily Andrew deserves pride of place as my editor and instigator. She came across my faculty webpage, saw a description of my simulation, and thought the subject might make for an interesting book. You are holding the result of a long and happy collaboration. I would also like to express my appreciation for the comments and insights offered by my anonymous readers. I hope they will be pleased with the results.

Thank you all.

INTRODUCTION

There is a quiet revolution underway in how history is taught to undergraduates and high school students. This book hopes to make it a noisy one. If you are reading these lines, maybe you do too.

Using a historical simulation does not just engage students, it can excite them. They can't wait to come to class. Time in class passes in a blink. Many stay after class. Just as many communicate about the simulation long after class. Nearly all will remember their participation in a simulation long after the semester ends.

But simulations are not golden touchstones of pedagogical wonder. As with any other teaching tool, their use requires consideration of their role in your course, the appropriateness of their content to that course, and the fit between their roles and your students. Just as there can be those awkward moments when a regular class discussion session opens to thunderous silence, a simulation exercise can fall flat on its face as students refuse to take their simulated roles seriously, or at all.

This book hopes to serve as a guide for using simulations successfully in your teaching. I hope to show you how to find a simulation (or several) that fits your classes' needs—not just by providing a list of websites or resources where you can find hundreds of possible simulations already designed and packaged for classroom use. I want to help you be able to consider which of those simulations might be a good fit for you and for your students—things to think about when you evaluate possible simulations, ways to kick the tires. I also want to help you, and encourage you, to think about designing your own classroom simulation, and how to design one that will engage and excite your students (and avoid some mistakes I made along the way in the simulations that I have designed and used over the past thirty years).

To do so, I am going to refer often to four simulations. Three are drawn from the highly successful Reacting to the Past[1] project: *Greenwich Village, 1913: Suffrage, Labor, and the New Woman*; *The Trial of Galileo: Aristotelianism, the "New Cosmology," and the Catholic Church, 1616–1633*; and *Stages of Power, Marlowe and Shakespeare, 1592*. The fourth is my own design: *Great Power Rivalries, 1936–1947*.

I have chosen the three Reacting to the Past examples to illustrate some important points. First, simulations are not the same as war games. Sims can recreate historical episodes that do not involve violence, although most successful simulations will have conflict in them, things that force students to advocate, debate, and choose sides. Second, simulations can and do span centuries. They are not bound to the recent past. Third, simulations can be very brief, requiring just a few class sessions, or, as with my *Rivalries*, very long, spanning an entire semester. Just as you tailor lectures or select readings to fit your needs, you will want to pick—or design—a simulation that is the right fit for you and your students. Another possibility is to pick and then modify an existing simulation, expanding or, more often, contracting it to get that fit. Here, too, this book should help point the way.

Simulations: Can High School Teachers Use Them?

This last option—modification of a simulation—is important. A quick perusal of most available simulations, whether from the Reacting to the Past consortium or any of the other sites mentioned in this book, will reveal that they are written for collegiate teaching. Simulations generally require a good deal of preparation time for students, not just teachers. A central feature of the *Galileo* simulation, for example, requires a good understanding of the nature of science, astronomy, and physics of Galileo's time. It is not meant for STEM majors, but rather incorporates learning about these subjects as part of the simulation itself. Fair enough, but perhaps ambitious for some younger students.

Consideration of the moral and ethical complications of role-playing historical characters in simulations is a factor as well, one that is frankly difficult to modify your way around. My *Rivalries* has to include Nazi Germany in its universe, so it has to include Hitler and other Nazis. I devote much time and space below to discussing these complications. Here, it is enough to say that some younger students might be too, well, young to be able to handle such situations.

But that is no reason to rule simulations out entirely in high school teaching. The great majority of simulations can treat sensitive subjects—as *Greenwich Village* does in the case of the role of women, for example—in ways that students can relate to and engage with. *Greenwich Village* itself might be too long, or require too much reading, for the needs of a high school course, perhaps. But a modified version of it could be ideal. As a teacher, you just have to keep focus on what you want in a simulation—off-the-shelf, modified, or designed yourself.

My Approach: How This Book Is Organized

To these ends, this book opens with a discussion of how games work generally, and what good simulation designers or teachers will incorporate into the games that they use. Whether you are custom building your own simulation for use in your own teaching environment, or whether you have decided to try (or modify) off-the-shelf simulations, already designed, organized, and ready with readings and assignments, this discussion highlights things you should think about before kicking things off. I want to show you the flexibility and range of classroom simulations. I want to prove that simulations need not be simple war games or, for that matter, simple at all.

Chapter 2 focuses on the key role of roles. A central aspect—and attraction—of simulations is their ability to make history personal for students by having them assume the roles of actual, composite, or plausible historical characters. Students will step into the shoes of Galileo, or belong to a Shakespearian theater company, or find themselves in New York's Greenwich Village in 1913, or represent Stalin or Hitler or Churchill. The proper choice, formation, and use of historical roles is overwhelmingly important in any simulation.

Students do not just assume roles. They interact with each other, often intensively, over the course of a simulation. Those interactions can be fairly tightly scripted, or they may be quite flexible. No matter where on this spectrum they fall, however, student interactions need to be governed by rules that ensure order in the class session and, as importantly, reinforce the students' sense of being in their characters' roles.

Games are meant to be fun. Classroom simulations are no exception, a key reason why students enjoy them so much. But they are serious academic exercises, too. Simulations have assignments and tasks, preparing and delivering presentations, doing research and writing about roles beyond the background materials offered in the simulation's introductory kit, mastering the historical context of one's character. What should be considered in making these assignments provides the subject for chapter 4.

If a simulation asks students to represent, to become, historical actors, it should also provide a suitable stage for them. Instructors have always known that the size and layout of the classroom can pivotally affect the teaching and learning that occurs within it. Simulations are no exception. Within the limits of the possible, simulation instructors need to think about what room basics and enhancements might be possible to contribute to a more encouraging and effective simulation environment.

The role and purpose of the instructor concerns chapter 6. Simulations cede much of the class session to the students. It is entirely possible and even likely that the instructor need be little more than an observer. But there are still things that require attention and, on occasion, intervention. One of the most important is a class session allowing students to reflect upon their simulation experiences once the game itself concludes. Student postmortems often provide not just a summary, but often the epitome, of student learning experiences.

These first six chapters are all you need to start running simulations in your class. But if you want more detail on how to write, design, and invent your own custom simulation, chapters 7, 8, and 9 offer my own experiences and lessons. In chapter 9, I conclude with a brief excursion into a key factor that makes simulations exciting: the students' drives to see if they can "do better" than their historical counterparts. Can you, as Galileo, persuade the Catholic Church to adopt some of your ideas? Can you, as Marlowe, become more famous than Shakespeare as the best playwright of Elizabethan theater? Can you, as Churchill, save not just Britain but the British Empire? Can you, in short, beat Churchill?

If this small book encourages or enables you to try simulations as a way to teach, it will not only have served its purpose. It will, as you will see, also bring a liveliness and excitement to your students, one of the best rewards a teacher has to offer, and to enjoy.

1

From Game to Simulation

History did not lead me to games. Games led me to history.

I was about ten years old and my mother had dragged me along on a shopping trip to the local Woolworth's. I hated these expeditions, much preferring to cavort on the backyard swing set or enjoy a round of tag football with the other boys in the neighborhood. But as we entered the five-and-dime, I saw two colorful boxes. One bore the name "Gettysburg," the other "U-Boat." Seeing no store clerks in the area, I pried them open, to discover a bewildering array of counters, mounted boards, and rule books nearly as thick as anything I had seen in my classes at Penn Street Elementary. I had stumbled upon the infant industry of commercial war games and I was hooked.

It was a craving that had to wait a few months. The games cost five dollars each. My weekly allowance was twenty-five cents. Swift calculations demonstrated that Christmas would be arriving sooner than any effort to save up, so I plotted how to best convince my mother that I'd much rather have a board game than an Etch A Sketch or erector set. So began my war game collection.

War-gaming itself is centuries old. Chess, Go, Chaturanga—these span centuries and cultures. But these earliest games were generic: white against black on simple, abstract game boards. War games like *Gettysburg* were different and more intriguing. *Gettysburg* pitted blue against gray, but did so in three fundamentally different ways. First, the forces given to each side were different, asymmetrical. Second, they were different because they were based on actual history. Northern cavalry arrives near the seminary north of town as Southern infantry approaches in the distance— just like the real battle. The challenge for each side is to do better than its historical counterpart. Which raises the third difference: historical war games blared—right on their box tops—You are there! You are Robert E. Lee, or George Meade! Step into their shoes (or boots) and see if you can do better.

This was heady stuff for someone still in grade school. Games like these triggered an intense interest to study the history behind them, to the amusement and occasional amazement of my teachers. But the more I read about history, the less enchanted I became with my war games. They were still plenty fun to play, especially during those rainy afternoons when nothing else beckoned. But I came to understand that games like *Gettysburg* or *U-Boat* really did a very poor job of making you a Lee or Meade, or the captain of a German submarine or British destroyer hunting it.

Lee would have given an arm, or maybe even a chunk of his army, to have the kind of panoramic view of the battlefield afforded the war-gamer. Perfect knowledge of the terrain, perfectly accurate information about the enemy's exact size, disposition, and location, assurances that one's own reinforcements would arrive at this precise time and that exact place—all of these have far more in common with chess or Go than any historical skirmish, battle, or war ever fought, much less the murk and uncertainty that plagued German subs or British sub-hunters. War games have a notoriously difficult time replicating what is known as the "fog of war."

Nor is this the only problem. When Lee the war-gamer dispatches orders to his troops, they do exactly as he says: move to location X and attack enemy formation Y at exactly the same time and in perfect coordination with another unit being given similar instructions. Of course, war-gamer Lee never issues instructions. He simply picks up the game counters, moves them as he wishes, and executes the attack, usually by rolling some dice. History's Lee, however, did dispatch orders. Some arrived late, others not at all, and every one of them was subject to the interpretation of his subordinate commanders and that fog of war. Maybe the other units in the coordinated attack arrived late, or early, and no coordination took place at all. Maybe the local commander was cautious in executing his instructions, or overly zealous. Maybe he just took a wrong turn. No matter how scrupulous and painstaking the research behind them, historical war games cannot hope to approach a true replication of actual historical conditions.

Including the most vital condition of all: victory. Open the rules booklet to any war game, whether chess or *Gettysburg* or any other, and you will invariably see a section clearly defining "victory conditions," how to determine who wins. In chess, each player strives to achieve checkmate. The condition is simple and unambiguous. In *Gettysburg* things are not. To be sure, the game's rules can define victory in a number of ways. If Lee captures a certain location by a certain time, he wins. If he inflicts more losses than he suffers, he wins. Or maybe if he just survives the battle with a certain number of his own troop counters on the board, he wins.

Any of these conditions would be unambiguous and satisfy the gamer at the table. There may be some dim, attenuated connection between learning to win a chess match and commanding troops successfully on the battlefield, but the object of a chess player, whether novice or grand master, is to find a way to win. Gaining insights into the background, context, and motivations of the white queen or black rook is simply not a consideration. *Gettysburg* would seem to be better in this regard, but that game's victory conditions are defined in order to let a player win—to let the game end—in a reasonably and entertainingly short period of time, not worry about what comes next for Lee or anyone else.

But history's Lee was not sitting at a gaming table on a rainy afternoon. He may not have been even interested in taking a given location or inflicting more losses or surviving the battle he was about to fight. In fact, history's Lee was all too aware that, up until those fateful days of July 1863, he had won, or at least drawn, every major battle he had ever fought. For Lee, for anyone fighting for the South, battlefield victories were, in themselves, meaningless unless they contributed in some way to what the South itself defined the real victory condition of its war: the North's recognition of its independence, without further interference in maintaining the institution of human slavery, and the North's ceasing its attempts to force the South back into the Union.

Simulating this actual victory condition poses real problems for a game on the battle of Gettysburg. Some might feel demanding that they be addressed at all is an undue and unfair burden for such a game. Yet why was Lee at Gettysburg in the first place? He had taken his army north, as he had tried to do a year earlier, in order to bring the scourge of war to the people of Pennsylvania, to demoralize them and have them press the Northern government for peace, a peace that would recognize Southern independence. Or, if that government refused to do so, to elect a new government that would.

Gettysburg might be a terrific game. But if we were designing it as a way to teach history, how would Lee's actual, historical victory conditions translate into a player's victory in the game? How would we begin to really make a student-Lee understand the wider considerations involved as the battle began? Like games, college courses end, and we cannot expect a simulation of Gettysburg to go on for a year or more afterward. But we do have to design a simulation of that battle in a way to give its participants a sense of what happens next to their characters depending on the simulation's outcome. Clearly, Lee has to emerge from the battle with an army sufficiently intact to continue its march through Pennsylvania. Ideally, it will be able to continue that march unopposed or at least unhindered by a Northern army. So it would make sense to define our game victory conditions in two tiers. Lee will have to retain a certain number of his own troops intact by battle's end. And he must inflict sufficient losses on the North to compel Meade's army to lick its wounds for the remainder of the summer and autumn.

But exactly how many should Lee have to retain? How many Northern losses are sufficient? No amount of historical research will answer these questions. Lee lost the battle, left Pennsylvania, and never returned. There is no historical record suggesting what he might have accomplished had he won.

This lack of record explains why many historians are uncomfortable with simulations. They force consideration of might-have-beens, not just "weres." But unless these other outcomes are considered, history becomes a mere time line. Event A had to happen pretty much the way it did, lead-ing to event B, then C, and so on. The South might as well have surren-dered before even firing on Fort Sumter. It was preordained to lose.

History as time line is simple, but it is simply bad history. Most histori-ans of the US Civil War do not consider a Northern victory as inevitable. Even if the South proved unable to mount a sustained invasion of the North, many accounts note that various outside powers, especially Great Britain, were either interested in dampening the growing dominance over North America by the United States or appalled by the tremendous loss of life that the early battles had led to. It was hardly improbable that Britain might have offered, or even insisted on, a mediated end to the war, either one of which would have put Lincoln in a difficult position, especially if Britain indicated a willingness to disregard the North's naval blockade of the South. As well, even with the war situation evolving as it did, there was substantial sentiment among the Northern public to end the fighting, as Lincoln's reelection campaign in 1864 demonstrates. Like it or not, his-tory is contingent. It could have turned out quite differently. Simulations, in forcing us to consider these possibilities, make us better historians.

One such historian was Ernest R. May, my doctoral adviser. May was not in the war games business, nor did he design simulations, but he wrote histories that emphasized the contingent nature of our past. His *Making of the Monroe Doctrine* emphasized how the United States ought to have accepted Britain's offer of de facto alliance in 1823.[1] Every senior policy maker and former president favored doing so. Only Secretary of State John Quincy Adams favored rejection, sure that acceptance would tar him as a lackey of London and doom his own presidential hopes in the 1824 election. May's study was an example of how an unlikely outcome became the actual one.

There are not any games on the making of the Monroe Doctrine (though you should be able to devise one after reading this book), but there are hundreds on the various aspects of the Second World War. Here, too, May had something to say about the role of contingency in history. The opening section of his study, *Strange Victory*, reads:

> If leaders in the Allied governments had anticipated the German offensive through the Ardennes, even as a worrisome contingency, it is almost in-conceivable that France would have been defeated when and as it was. It is

more than conceivable that the outcome would have been not France's defeat but Germany's and, possibly, a French victory parade on the Unter den Linden in Berlin.[2]

May goes on to observe that France had an excellent intelligence network and should have been prepared for the contingency of Germany's offensive through the Ardennes forest, as actually happened. He dismisses the usual explanations for France's defeat: poor weaponry, poorer leadership, and a public with no stomach for fighting. None hold water.

Although May was not in the simulations business himself, he was well aware that when he was writing *Strange Victory*, at the height of the Cold War between the United States and the Soviet Union, the US government, especially the US military, was deeply interested in war-gaming. The chief arena of its concern was a hypothetical Soviet invasion of West Germany. Could US and Allied forces hold or at least delay the Soviet advance before it reached the heavily populated and industrialized cities along the Rhine, or at least before the Russians reached the French border? The US military had quite detailed war games, far more detailed than *Gettysburg*, but it had no way of knowing how accurately they mirrored reality since, obviously, there had never been an actual Soviet invasion to test things on.

There was no way to test the accuracy of the Pentagon's models for a Soviet invasion in the 1980s, perhaps. But why not adjust a few variables and see if those models, given inputs for Germany and France in 1940, could accurately simulate Germany's crushing, six-week victory over France? The Pentagon commanded vast resources, including the assistance of (for the time) high-powered computers that would allow not only sound adjustments for things like quality of guns, speed of march, and so on, but also the replaying of the German invasion dozens or even hundreds of times relatively quickly.

The results of these war games were highly disturbing to the US military. France defeated Germany most of the time. In fact, to replicate Germany's historical success, Germany had to be given arbitrary (and ahistorical) advantages—the proverbial thumb on the scale. Did these results mean that the war-gaming model was flawed? May didn't think so and, in part, wrote *Strange Victory* to vindicate the model and show that France's actual defeat was not due to poor hardware, bad leaders, or the French public's lack of spine.

May conceded that the last of these three factors was the most difficult to demonstrate. How do you gauge the mood of the public? Its determination or war-weariness? There are some clear indicators in extreme circumstances, such as the Bolshevik Revolution or French army mutiny, both in 1917. The collapse of South Vietnam in 1975 or the Batista regime in Cuba in 1958 might be others. But even in these cases it is difficult to isolate the "public mood" as a key variable.

It should come as no surprise that, just as historians consider public support gingerly, designers of historical war games usually avoid the subject altogether. Indeed, the wider, political contexts of the struggles portrayed in the vast majority of war games are likewise ignored. No game on the battle of Gettysburg pays mind to the role of British observers and what they might relay to their government in London, with potentially decisive consequences for the wider war. A superb re-creation of the complexities of getting Civil War armies to coordinate their battlefield actions exists in Dean Essig's marvelous Civil War Brigade Series of games, which started with an examination of the battle of Antietam. These are far better studies of the past than my childhood experience with *Gettysburg*. For all that, even this series contents itself with battlefield results in its calculations of victory conditions. The missed opportunities are legion. Essig's game on the battle of Perryville, Kentucky, is superbly researched and drawn, but passes over the possibility that a decisive Southern victory in it would have lost Kentucky for the Union and, as Abraham Lincoln acknowledged, probably lost the Union the war as well.

This sort of insulation from wider political and social factors is hardly confined to games on the US Civil War. Wading through literally thousands of games on the various battles of the Second World War—by far the most popular subject for war games—will produce a bare handful that consider politics and publics at all. The most popular subjects of this most popular war are not the actions that could have affected the wider struggle's outcome most directly. There are surprisingly few games on Operation Typhoon, Germany's push to capture Moscow in late 1941, but nearly a hundred on the battle of Stalingrad, where even a crushing German victory (historically unlikely) would not have altered the overall outcome of the war as much. There are dozens of war games covering the entire Eastern (Soviet) front of the war, from 1941 to 1945. Some are excellent military re-creations. Not one treats the extermination of civilians (Jews and others) in captured territory with anything approaching seriousness, despite the Nazis' clear objective that, in many regards, this was a primary reason for invading the Soviet Union in the first place.

Skirting political and civilian constraints and concerns might be understandable for games on the Second World War, a "total war" that saw its contestants seldom give quarter. But most wars are not total, and one might expect some degree of political considerations in games about them. One obvious case would be the US war in Vietnam from 1965 to 1975. From the time the first combat troops waded ashore until today, some people in the United States have blamed political limits on waging that war, especially concerning the use of airpower, as responsible for the loss of South Vietnam. Others have participated in, and point with pride to, antiwar demonstrations that, they argue, were responsible for the eventual US withdrawal from an unwinnable war. There are few games on the US war in Vietnam. Even the best of them, such as *Fire in the Lake: Insurgency in Vietnam* by Mark Herman and Volko Ruhnke,[3] confine themselves to battles in South Vietnam. The effects of the US bombing campaign against the North are not major factors. There is no option for a ground invasion of the North. Nor much consideration of the ongoing and worsening ineffectiveness of whichever regime held nominal power in Saigon (though the game does take into account regime change there, usually through military coup).

In games, these omissions are understandable and even necessary. Games may well illustrate some aspects of their subjects. They may illuminate, educate, and stimulate players to find out more about those subjects. But their primary purpose is to be played, nearly always by two people if not always on that hypothetical rainy afternoon. Two people, and playable start-to-finish in that afternoon or, at a stretch, over a long weekend. And it is rather difficult to find larger groups of people willing and able to devote sufficient time to playing together.

One result is that outstanding games that require true multiplayer participation are rarely ever played.[4] In this sense, games are a kind of two-dimensional exercises for three- or four- or five-dimensional realities. Some game designers recognize as much and incorporate ingenious mechanisms to take those extra dimensions into account. *Fire in the Lake* allows participation of four players. The North Vietnamese Army and

National Liberation Front (Viet Cong) are allied but with differing, sometimes conflicting, objectives, as are the United States and the Army of the Republic of (South) Vietnam. The designers understand that gathering four players, with a customary play time of four to six hours, will be difficult. So their game offers "flow sheets" to dictate automatic actions for any faction not represented by a human, a sort of paper artificial intelligence. The result does a good job of representing the dummy faction, but has the somewhat dreary effect of compelling the real humans to spend even more time running the dummies through their turns. A necessary but tedious exercise, albeit one that begins to approach the perspective of a multifaceted, role-playing simulation.

But what if you could create an environment in which many players were possible? Not just three or four, but perhaps up to ten, thirty, or more? And an environment in which all of those players could afford to spend four to six hours, or even considerably more, together? What if you could create an environment in which real historical simulation, encompassing a dozen or even dozens of perspectives and objectives, would be possible? This environment already exists: the classroom.

When I first started offering *Great Power Rivalries*, students flocked to it and responded with an enthusiasm that literally spread through the hallways of my department. But my colleagues, at first, were dismissive. Of course students liked it. It was just a "game," easy entertainment, not a serious way to learn history. But historical simulations are far more than games. They can be deep and complex. They can easily involve many participants, and easily span four to six hours or, as *Great Power Rivalries* does, an entire semester, about forty hours of class time. Many outcomes are possible, not just win-or-lose, not just learning history as a simple time line. Students in classroom simulations take a stake in remaking history, creating a world themselves. To do so, they drive themselves to learn about their characters and, for the really good students, to learn about others' characters to better manipulate them.

My students motivated themselves to learn history. My colleagues, in time, came to understand this motivation: that students in my simulation worked as hard to understand the history in the simulation as any of their students did in a more traditional course, probably much harder. Some began to ask me if they might try to use simulations in their classes. I encouraged them, but most became discouraged when they realized that composing a simulation involves as much preparation as writing a scholarly article, or even a book.

There is no escaping the fact that composing a simulation is work, plenty of it. And preparing a simulation requires different steps compared to standard academic activities: writing lectures or articles.[5] Making the work of actually designing your own simulation easier, and the still easier task of understanding how best to run or modify a simulation already designed, are what we are after here. Using *Great Power Rivalries* and other simulations designed by other professional historians as examples, let's walk through the key considerations and components of any classroom simulation meant to teach history by having students remake it.

Key Components of a Simulation: A Deeper Look

The first key component is who the students will be: their *roles*. These need to be specific, historically accurate, and selected to maximize student engagement. Above all, they have to make clear to the students representing them how to act—what goals to pursue, what means are available to pursue those goals. For great power rivalries from 1936 to 1947, should we have Chamberlain or Churchill representing Britain? Do we need a student representing Poland, or is this a role that will be twiddling its thumbs fruitlessly most of the time? A simulation of the trial of Galileo will need a Galileo, and a pope, but who else, and why them? Do we want Marlowe and Shakespeare to present their cases directly to the Queen? Or should their companies do so to a broad, multifactioned Privy Council? Greenwich Village in 1913 was a swirl of different groups, each with ideas and hopes for their futures. How many should be represented? For how many of these can the simulation offer enough material for eager student researchers? The various Reacting to the Past simulations do not specify an exact number of participants, understanding that course enrollments (and instructor proclivities) will vary. So even if you are using an already-published simulation, it is worthwhile to consider the fit of students to roles. If you are designing your own simulation, you can custom-fit it to your class and your students.

Once students' roles have been determined, what they will clash over must be. For many simulations, especially those that will occupy only a few class sessions, the *points and means of contention*—otherwise known as rules—can be nearly as straightforward as those of chess or Go. Will Galileo be excommunicated or not? Will his theories be suppressed or tolerated? Is Marlowe's play going to be put on or Shakespeare's, or neither's? There needs to be a purpose for each role. Establishing points of contention establishes purpose.

For briefer simulations, these points are fairly straightforward. Whatever other interactions there might be among students, all will be focused on the climactic trial of Galileo, or a decision between Shakespeare and Marlowe. Longer and more complex simulations require more thought. *Greenwich Village* has multiple possible outcomes. "Sandbox" simulations like *Great Power Rivalries* are even more open ended. These kinds of simulations need more comprehensive yet clear sets of procedures governing student interactions. And they need to do so in ways that will encourage students to ask questions—to learn—about their characters and the world those characters lived in. If proper selection of student roles is the foundation of a good simulation, clear descriptions and guidelines of how those roles interact—the simulation's rules—are its streets and paths.

Next discussed is the social nature of class simulations. No student is an island, or at least no student should be. It can be daunting, even depressing, to sit, alone to oneself, in a traditional lecture course or even a recitation/discussion section where your interaction, if any, consists of asking a question of the lecturer or being asked one by the section leader. Students will form study groups themselves to make learning course material easier, or at least more bearable, and instructors have known for a long time that team learning works well, at least in boosting student morale and sometimes with real learning results. Online courses try to mimic this effect through discussion boards. Whatever the nature of the course, it can nearly always be improved by introducing students to each other, compelling them to talk with each other during every minute of every class. And not only talk. In many simulations, students have to act together. They have to cooperate to reach mutual objectives. They have to build a team, even when the individual goals of their various roles are not perfectly aligned. This need for cooperation often leads them to continue their discussions long after class has concluded. Late-night or early-morning emails, messaging, or coffee shop face-to-face time are typical, not the exception, when a simulation is in progress.

Simulations lend themselves to this happy outcome through their very nature. All have factions or teams. How to construct those teams is another crucial element in designing a simulation. How many student roles should be on each team? How closely aligned should each student's role be with the team that student belongs to? Put another way, how harmonious within itself should a team be?

Students will not just interact with teammates. Teams will compete against each other. The manner and nature of that competition needs to be designed itself. Another compelling reason to take care in designing or understanding a simulation's rules. There must be ways to adjudicate differences. Some simulations have a final, deciding vote, whether within a papal council over Galileo's fate or a royal or Privy Council edict for a play's production. Other simulations, such as *Great Power Rivalries*, have an array of competitions, from a quest for diplomatic influence or decisions over national team budgets to actual manipulation of armies and fleets. Simple or complex, the rules need to be understandable and students need to see them as fair.

Especially in simulations, the perception of fairness is paramount. Students have to see the instructor's evaluations of their simulation performances as balanced and evenhanded. Achieving this objective is not easy. In a conventional course, fairness seems obvious. Every student hears the same lectures, is assigned the same reading, and takes the same examination. But in a simulation, every student has a different starting position, different tools available, different assignments required, and different goals, some of which conflict with those of other students. Some have longer races than others, or higher hurdles. How can *grading* seem or be fair?

Roles, rules, teams, and conflicting goals can make for conflicted students, especially those who are shy by nature. If the essence of a classroom simulation is to learn by doing—by remaking history—what is to be done with students who are intrinsically introverted, jaded by the usual classroom model of take notes and regurgitate same, or simply terrified of performing before their peers? *Engaging* students is at the core of any simulation, but it does not happen on its own. Nor can it be forced. Students are not ciphers. They have their own backgrounds, experiences, and sensitivities that have to be acknowledged in ways much deeper than traditional courses can allow. To use the most obvious examples: a simulation set in the United States before the Civil War will compel its students to grapple with slavery, perhaps even slaves. One set in 1930s Europe is going to have Nazi Germany, and Nazis, to deal with. These issues must be addressed with care.

As noted in my introduction, throughout this book I refer to a number of simulations to illustrate these points. It's time to introduce them in some detail:

Greenwich Village, 1913

Greenwich Village, 1913: Suffrage, Labor, and the New Woman, composed by Mary Jane Treacy and published in the Reacting to the Past series by W. W. Norton, puts students in the Greenwich Village area of New York City in 1913.[6] In particular, its activities center around a small restaurant/salon named Polly's, near Washington Square. Some student characters are real, like Emma Goldman, Crystal and Max Eastman, Randolph Bourne, and Mabel Dodge, the de facto concertmaster at Polly's. Others are composite or hypothetical personages.

Regardless of their backgrounds, all student characters have strong views on the issues of the day. Should women have the right to vote? To seek divorce? To have their own identities independent of their husbands, or even on their own as single by choice? Should workers be able to strike without fear of violence from employer-hired goons, or from the police? Should strikers be able to occupy company property and shut down the owners' operations entirely?

Debates, sometimes structured in a specifically scheduled class session, sometimes freewheeling among the students, propose different answers to these questions. But they are all designed to culminate in a final class that has a vote among the student-characters as to whether they will join a suffragist parade or the Industrial Workers of the World (IWW)–sponsored Paterson Silk Strike pageant (or neither, or form yet a third demonstration). Some characters have their positions fixed on this question. Many do not and are open to persuasion. They can persuade, too, by a wide variety of means from writing pamphlets of their own to sporting clothing in class in suffragist colors or labor style. Students raising their characters' profiles through participating in sloganeering, song, or writing and directing a skit at Polly's, among other activities, will see their final votes assigned greater weight. Certain characters, such as Max Eastman or Emma Goldman, begin the simulation with broad public reputations and considerable influence over the final vote.

Stages of Power

Stages of Power: Marlowe and Shakespeare, 1592, designed by Eric Mallin and Paul Sullivan, has been published by the Reacting Consortium Press.[7] It pits two rival acting companies, each associated with two rival playwrights, against each other for the right to perform the first play upon the reopening of London theaters after the plague had closed them in 1592. A third set of student-characters, representing Queen Elizabeth's interests and their own, will render a decision after class presentations, stagings and debates. There is one neutral or "indeterminate" role in the person of Eleanor Bull, a tavern owner. The two companies are aligned with the established playwright Christopher Marlowe, who hopes to stage his *Tragical History of Dr. Faustus*, and a rising star, William Shakespeare, who has penned *Richard III*. Both plays touch upon controversial political subjects, especially concerning the English crown, and the Queen's councillors will have to be mindful of the impact on the public from either being shown.

The Trial of Galileo

Also published by the Reacting Consortium Press, and coauthored by Frederick Purnell Jr., Michael Pettersen, and Mark Carnes, *The Trial of Galileo: Aristotelianism, the "New Cosmology," and the Catholic Church, 1616–1633* spans the Catholic Church's initial inquiries about the famous astronomer's work in 1616 and his trial, which ran from 1623 to 1633.[8]

The simulation pivots around the trial, but offers plenty of subplots. At stake is not just whether Galileo is guilty of heresy. The characters also have to determine if his work should be suppressed, what his punishment might be, and, not least, whether his theories about the earth's place in the cosmos are right. Ultimately each of these questions is answered by the pope, who himself has to worry about defending the Catholic Church against the rising threat of Protestantism regardless of the merits of anyone's case. But a panel of church cardinals will offer advice to these ends, and the debates over the questions will be guided by three broad groups. The conservatives seek harsh measures against Galileo and his work. Moderates are willing to accept his scientific findings so long as they can be reconciled with Holy Scripture. Linceans (after a famous scientific academy founded in 1603) mean to argue that God is manifest in science, and science may be a more reliable guide to his cosmos than a literal reading of the Bible.

Great Power Rivalries

I will also draw on my own *Great Power Rivalries, 1936–1947* to provide examples demonstrating the key concepts involved in designing or using a classroom simulation. *Rivalries* is a sprawling, semester-long affair. It is not ideal for an instructor's first try at simulations in the classroom and it is not necessary for anyone to master it in order to understand how to design shorter, simpler, but no less successful simulations for the classroom. But it does provide a deep look into how simulations are assembled.

Now to the beginning: casting the roles.

2

Roles

The role's the thing.

In any simulation designed to teach, but especially in history simulations, it is impossible to overstate the importance of getting the roles right. Each student must represent her or his historical character as faithfully as time and resources allow. It is like being an actor. It is not enough just to read the script. Good actors understand their roles, ideally become their roles. For students, this understanding is even more vital, because there is no set script. There are only episodes—class sessions—that might follow a general pattern but are improvised in practically all specifics.

Getting into their roles is the students' responsibility. Defining which roles should be in the simulation at all is the instructors'. Sometimes, this definition is straightforward. *The Trial of Galileo* must have a Galileo. But then things get fuzzier. Should the pope be a role, or should he be "off-screen" and simply advised by a papal council of several student-characters? If the latter, how many such characters, and should they be real personages or just composite cardinals or archbishops? Is Galileo to be alone in confronting the church, or should he have sympathetic allies? If so, allies from the scientific community, the more reform-minded clergy, or both? Should these be real people or composites?

Greenwich Village complicates the selection of roles even further. Mabel Dodge, for example, seems necessary. But the Greenwich Village of 1913 had a bewilderingly large number of personages who wandered through, and there is no single historical event forcing focus, as there is in *Galileo*'s trial. Here the instructor's choices of roles will critically affect all other aspects of the simulation. *Stages of Power* falls between *Galileo* and *Greenwich Village*. It has a defining event (whose play will be performed?), but considerable flexibility concerning roles. Should Marlowe and Shakespeare be represented directly? Should the queen herself have a role? Or should the playwrights' companies and royal representatives, representing the queen's Privy Council, be at center?

Class Size and the Number of Roles

In an ideal world, you would design your simulation with exactly the roles you need to make its dynamics work. The actual number of students in your class would have to conform to the number of roles you have deemed ideal. *Great Power Rivalries* does just this because it can. It is a semester-long seminar that my university allows me to cap at thirty-five students, exactly the number of roles I have set for it. And I can fill those thirty-five seats because I have a surplus of students who want to enroll.

Few other instructors, or simulation designers, will enjoy this luxury. Among other factors, few other simulations will run for the entire semester. They will instead be incorporated into courses with their enrollments driven by other considerations. Some of these courses might be small seminars of a dozen or half dozen students. Others could be quite large courses primarily using a lecture or lecture/recitation format. In any event, the numbers of students and ideal simulation roles will not match up. What then?

A handy list of classroom simulations in various stages of development and use can be found at the BLORG (Big List of Reacting Games) on the website of the Reacting to the Past simulation consortium.[1] Among other things, the Big List notes the number of class sessions a simulation runs (anywhere from one for the *Jumonville Incident, 1754*, to the nearly forty of my *Great Power Rivalries*; most average between three and six sessions) and how many "players" or roles the simulation calls for. Here, the range extends from a low of six, for *Embers of Intrigue: A Prelude to the 1741 New York Slave Conspiracy*, to over a hundred, in the case of *The US Response to the Ebola Outbreak, 2014–2015*. Nearly all give a range of roles, typically from one to two or three dozen.

One to three dozen is a congenial number for many courses or recitation sections or high school classes, but it does raise questions about larger, usually lecture-style, courses that enroll forty students or more. For these, the least attractive option is to have some students participate while the rest observe. Being cut out of the action is neither fun nor fair, and raises obvious questions about how those who participate in the simulation will have their course grades affected compared to those who do not. Running a sim serially, where one portion of the class participates while another observes, then vice versa, solves some of these problems but extends the number of class sessions the sim requires. Running two or more simulations simultaneously is likely to tax the instructor's time and resources. In cases where the simulation requires constant instructor observation or intervention, parallel simulations become practically impossible.

One factor allowing some simulations to be quite flexible in the number of roles for students is whether they are to play actual historical characters or any number of generic, composite personages who did not exist, by name, in the episode being simulated but who might have participated even if history does not recall their names or actual backgrounds and dispositions. Especially if you are designing your own simulation, you will need to consider the pros and cons of using composites.[2]

Real or Composite Roles?

Any role that you decide to incorporate into your simulation needs to be fleshed out. The customary vehicle for doing so is through *role sheets*, discussed in the section immediately following this one.

Using an actual person from history in your simulation has a number of distinct advantages. At the top is the student's ability to identify with their character. To see a photograph or drawing, to read the words of a person who once lived and made a mark on history, these are powerful experiences for the student. They are also useful materials for the preparation of those role sheets, real primary sources. Students will work hard and diligently try to stay in character. What would Galileo or Edward Alleyn or Mabel Dodge or Winston Churchill have done?

Composite characters have their uses too. Their biggest edge stems from their flexibility in numbers and relative ease of preparation. Nicolas Proctor and Margaret Storey's *Kentucky, 1861*[3] is a splendid example. It uses primary sources from actual historical characters, but moves each into a category that can accommodate a highly flexible number of composite or generic players in that category. Henry Clay is a Constitutional Unionist, for instance, obviously opposing Kentucky's secession. Other historical figures are used as material for the secessionist or neutral factions. Using composites allows for great flexibility in creating factions too. *Kentucky, 1861* revolves around the question of secession, but other issues and therefore other interests are in play as well, such as anti-immigration feelings of immediate concern to the Louisville Banker faction. Utilizing composite characters works particularly well if the instructor has prepared the students' various role sheets before the simulation begins, as those sheets can be written to articulate clear positions concerning exactly those issues the instructor wants the students to focus on. In addition, writing role sheets for real characters is a one-for-one proposition. For every character that will or could be in your simulation, you have to have a fully developed role sheet completed whether that character ends up being in play or not. For composite characters, one role sheet will do for whatever number of students you have representing that faction.

There are other excellent uses for composite characters. Besides allowing for considerable flexibility in how many students can participate in the simulation overall, composites can provide numerical balance for factions that otherwise would be badly outnumbered. They can also offer perspectives that are helpful for your simulation where real characters either did not exist at all, or left no records behind.

For example, *Galileo* can accommodate as few as fourteen or as many as thirty-two students by adding cardinals as necessary to the conservative, moderate, or Lincean (pro-Galileo) factions. *Stages* can distribute extras among the Privy Council, or Marlowe's or Shakespeare's acting companies. *Greenwich Village* has no composites as such, but does include a wide array of "villagers" allowing for variety in class size. Composites could be easily imagined and included.

Good cases of including composites to introduce different perspectives can be seen in a different Reacting simulation: *Frederick Douglass, 1845*, by Mark Higbee and James B. Stewart.[4] It focuses on the complex relationship between the institution of slavery, the Constitution, and the future of the Union. It features an impressive cast of actual characters: Elizabeth Cady Stanton, William Lloyd Garrison, and Douglass himself, to name only three. But it also has composites. The Ambitious Georgian is a young white, a successful slave overseer bent on becoming an independent plantation owner. He needs money, and has come to New York City (where the simulation is set) seeking ways to get it, ideally by striking a blow against the Northern abolitionists in the process. The Whiskey Dealer, also ambitious, is a Long Islander eager to introduce Kentucky bourbon to the big cities of the Northeast. It's time to make some Southern connections while avoiding complications with the temperance people.

Douglass also provides an example of a composite who can speak for those who left scant records behind. A Fugitive Slave Woman from Kentucky has fled master and family and begins the simulation working as a housemaid in New York. Her heart burns for revenge against slaveholders everywhere, but she is acutely aware that slave catchers routinely patrol the city's streets. Perhaps if she could make the acquittance of some of the more influential abolitionists?

With thought and care, the inclusion of composites can add both flexibility and spice to a simulation. But whether you employ composites or stick to actual characters, it is imperative to provide or provide for role sheets to guide the students throughout their simulation experience.

Role Sheets

Whether the instructor or the students write these role sheets depends upon your pedagogical objectives and how much time you have to achieve them. The great majority of historical simulations currently available provide their own role sheets, already prepared by the simulation designers, or offer materials for you to write your own. Instructor-written or instructor-provided role sheets save class time by allowing the students to jump into their roles almost instantly. They also can be written to facilitate students choosing their roles or instructors choosing for them. Nicolas Proctor's *Game Designer's Handbook* summarizes the utility of instructor-written role sheets pointedly:

> They are better written than student ones.
> They are better cited than student ones.
> They are better researched than student ones.
> They emphasize the parts of their roles most pertinent to the purposes of the simulation, rather than wasting time on peripheral material such as the character's childhood and schooling.[5]

These points may be freely conceded, yet a case can still be made for having students write their own role sheets, as I do in *Great Power Rivalries*. In a semester-long simulation, I have ample time for the students to get their self-written role sheets right and to learn good research skills while doing so. They might improve their writing skills too.

Even in a long simulation, it is important for the students to understand their characters as quickly as possible. I require a first draft of the role sheets from all students after the first week of classes. Students will rush for the wikis as soon as they are out of the door, and all will meet the deadline, usually with something resembling a crude pocket biography, just as Proctor predicts. So-and-so was born in such and such, had this many brothers and sisters, and so on. Given most students' very elementary understanding of their characters at the start of my simulation, I have to be alert for wildly out-of-character decisions by students during that first week. Then comes the often-painful read-through of the students' first tries at role sheets.

The long-term payoff, though, is significant. Most undergraduates, like most bad biographers, do not understand the difference between recounting their subjects' time lines and understanding them and their worlds. By semester's end, they do. Here is one of my student's recollections from his experience in *Great Power Rivalries*:

> I sat in the dimly lit room with the other Chinese commanders, contemplating my precarious position on the Asian continent. Reviewing my maps did not paint a very encouraging picture of my place in this splintered region.

To the north, I spied Soviet troops, with their Chinese lackey, Mao Zedong; and to the east lay the Japanese, pulling on the strings on their puppet, Chiang Kai-shek. I, on the other hand, was trapped in the mountains—penniless, and without troops or allies. If I were to survive, I would need to tread very carefully, appeasing the communists that lay to the north, the fascist slowly creeping from the east, as well as the British colonials ever so present just south of me. And appease I did, slowly building up my power base, until the moment was finally right to reclaim what was rightfully mine—China.

Historically, Wang Jingwei was a traitor during World War II. As such, this gave me the ability to play one as well, choosing the political ideology that best would serve my motives to end imperialism in China. Armed with manipulation and deceit (which is all I had, since I began the simulation without troops, land, or money), I set off to unify China in my name. Over the next few months I repeatedly entered into temporary truces, enacted policy options, and participated in aggressive diplomacy. However, there was one defining moment which would determine the legacy I left behind in this world; that was the day I reclaimed British Hong Kong.

Through a slightly bizarre series of events, I came to ally with Mussolini and the Italian regime. As strange as it may seem, such an alliance made me privy to the fascist plans to invade the British mainland. This allowed for me to take part in a coordinated strike, where I would attack British colonial forces in Asia at the same time. What did I get out of it, you might ask? While I was finally able to oust the western imperialists in Hong Kong, reuniting it with the rest of China, as well as helping parts of British India escape western imperialism. Let's just say that the attack wasn't as coordinated as I would have hoped, with my troops attacking British Commonwealth territories, while the British and mainland European teams were discussing an armistice. That weekend involved marathon negotiations with representatives from the British government in order to prevent a full out retaliatory attack. We were able to work out an agreement—one where I would get to keep Hong Kong if I returned Burma—but come that Monday, I found out the person I had been negotiating with did not have the power he thought he did. I was instead confronted by Anthony Eden, demanding the immediate return of Burma, as well as Hong Kong. Needless to say I wasn't very keen on such a deal, and ripped his written peace treaty in half (right in front of him), then left. I wasn't there when he returned to the room with the democratic teams, but from what I heard, he was far from amused. Luckily, after tempers died down on both sides, we were able to reach a bilateral treaty, cooling the fiery tensions on both sides.[6]

I should add that, in addition to writing and revising their role sheets over the course of the semester, each student kept a personal journal, usually in the first person. Most keep them years after the simulation concludes.

Having the students write their own role sheets does not ease the instructor's burdens. Writing one to three dozen role sheets yourself takes time, quite a lot of it. But working with each student to revise and refine the sheets they wrote requires at least as many hours. How often, though, do you get to spend one-on-one sit-down time with each student in your class on material they are deeply interested in?

Having students write their own role sheets has other advantages, too, if the simulation provides good incentives (besides a good grade) to do so. *Rivalries* offers students the chance to write their own Policy Options and see them incorporated into the simulation—so long as they can make a case that their character would push for the option and, of course, that the option is historically plausible. One student on the British team wrote an option for army conscriptions, demonstrating that his character sponsored it historically, and that it would be realistic to see Britain able to trade quality for quantity in its Army Points.

Students can also take issue with the instructor's reading of their character, provided they have done their research to back their claim. For some US Policy Options, I indicate roughly where each character might have stood on them. For one, school desegregation, I assigned Wendell Willkie a neutral position. Student-Willkie disagreed, pointing to her character's positions in his 1940 presidential campaign and subsequent acts until his untimely death four years later. Willkie, she argued, would have strongly supported desegregation and she was going to do so in the simulation. It was gratifying to see the correction.[7]

Assigning Roles

However many students you have in your simulation, and however well prepared the characters' role sheets might be, there remains the problem of getting a good fit between students and characters.

Getting "a good fit" demands knowing what that phrase means. If the main point of any classroom simulation is to get the students to become a

person in another time, another place, a different world, then what difference does it make which student gets which role?

Well, it does. Some roles demand skills that a student may be uncomfortable with. Some roles require goals, and simulation actions toward
those goals, that clash with a student's own outlook and disposition.
Those roles might even deeply upset students asked to play them. One
case would be an offering of *Frederick Douglass*, in which nonwhite students might be asked to play (very white) advocates of slavery. Another
example, from my *Great Power Rivalries*, would be a Jewish student, perhaps the granddaughter or grandson of a Holocaust survivor, chosen to
play Adolf Hitler. In the era of "trigger-alerts" and heightened sensitivities
to student identities, this might be a case of really going nuclear.

That some of my most successful student-Hitlers have in fact been Jewish does not offer a solution for a student who would object to playing him, or any other Nazi for that matter. Questions of identity aside,
student-Hitler's performance in the simulation will affect the entire class
profoundly. An able, talented, and dedicated student as Hitler almost always drives the dynamics of every other national team, not just the German one. A casual, inattentive, or simply mediocre Hitler almost always
means a quick and inglorious end to the thousand-year Reich and a very
different trajectory for the entire simulation over the entire semester. The
matter of a good fit turns out to be nearly as crucial as getting the initial
determination of roles correct.

So: who decides which student will represent which historical figure?

This is a crucial question. So it is somewhat surprising that many of the
published or prepared simulations available, from the Reacting to the Past
project, for instance, have precious little guidance in this regard. Proctor's
Game Designer's Handbook has a brief discussion on this point, citing a
suggestion from the designer of *Greenwich Village* that any simulation
take care to include roles deliberately accommodating different student
personalities and abilities. Good advice, to be sure, but advice that does
little to assist making the best match between student and role.

One option in making those matches is simple randomness. As your
first order of class business, let the students draw chits or paper strips with
the names of the character they will be for the balance of the semester.
This method has the element of fairness. It also invites disaster. It has no
checks on mismatches in cases of student personalities, sensitivities, or

interests. Students saddled with a character they hate from the start will not be contributing to a vigorous and enriching experience for all. Nor is there any allowance for student abilities. As I note above, putting an apathetic, overtaxed, or just plain poor student into the role of Hitler invites a bad time for everyone.

A second option is to assign the students their characters beforehand, based on your knowledge of each student's abilities and personalities. You could even give a questionnaire to students before the simulation begins tailored to determining a good fit, as the *Greenwich Village* designer in fact suggests in her materials. This approach can minimize mismatches. Seth Offenbach at Bronx Community College used this approach to good effect in the first simulation he ever attempted, *Chicago, 1968*, assigning roles based on his evaluations of his students to that point. It was a great success for both him and his students. Every student, even the poorer ones, did the readings. Everyone actively participated. Everyone learned.[8]

But role assignment-by-instructor has its own pitfalls. Nearly all classroom simulations will be planned and prepared before the semester begins. Nearly all instructors will not know nearly all their new students. Assigning roles by student grade point averages, majors, or years in school seems arbitrary, even capricious. Interviews (if the instructor has time) or questionnaires (if the students complete them honestly) can help, but even these can give false readings. One year, I had an exceptionally talented student in *Great Power Rivalries*. She had been in several of my courses already. She was a superb student. I was certain she would delve deeply into her character's background and render an excellent portrayal. But she was exceptionally shy and terrified of speaking even in small groups. Would she have made a good Hitler? I had my reservations, but the real point was that I doubted whether I had sufficient grounds for prejudging what she might do in the role. And this was for a student I knew well. One of the main drawing points of doing a simulation at all is to allow the students leeway to learn on their own. As important, if the instructor assigns roles, some students will feel that the instructor is punishing them before the class has even begun. Why did she get the Margaret Sanger role in *Greenwich Village* while I'm stuck with Henrietta Rodman, whoever Rodman is. I'm a poor apprentice printer and he's William Shakespeare?? She was assigned Galileo but I'm the real-world STEM wizard! Or, my favorite from my own simulation: I landed on the French team. We're doomed!

The method I have settled upon for *Great Power Rivalries* is not quite random, yet gives no direct power of assignment to the instructor. At the first class and as the first order of business, I assemble all the enrolled students—exactly thirty-five of them—and ask which ones want to be on the German team. Germany is, I have learned, the most popular choice for students, leading Britain and the United States. (Only a few outliers want the Soviet Union or Japan, and virtually no one desires France, Italy, or China.) All the students who *want* to be Nazis for the semester join me in a separate room. There, they blindly draw numbered chits. There are five positions on the German team. The student drawing the lowest number (#1 goes first, if #1 is drawn, in other words) picks any open position. The second lowest can choose from any of the remaining four positions, and so on. If a student has the power to pick but finds no attractive position left open, she or he may pass, return to the central room, and try his or her luck with a different nation. After all the German positions are filled, students left with the lousy chit draws must pass and try again with a different nation. The process continues, nation by nation, until all the character positions are filled, almost always with the "losers" (of successive chit draws) bemoaning the fates which have consigned them to France.

My method is not foolproof. It still yields foolish Hitlers on occasion. But it forces no one to be Hitler. It leaves no hard feelings among students. It even has the advantage of creating a sense of bonhomie among the students drawing France, "we all had miserable luck of the draw, but we are in this boat together." Shy students are not forced into hard-driving, high visibility roles. Practically every national team has its quiet coordinator or observer: Germany's Schacht, France's Blum, Britain's Halifax, and so on.

The Un-Buddy System

To be or not to be Hitler is not the sole problem in the matter of assigning roles, either. It is not unusual for student friends or cliques to sign up for the same course, but in a simulation the existence of these groups can create issues. What if four or five buddies approach you and request to be assigned roles on the same national team, for example? It would seem natural and perhaps harmless to grant their wish and look forward to a harmonious team for the balance of the simulation.

I never agree to such requests. My first reason is elementary fairness. If I grant any student request for a specific team, I must grant all such. So long as students abhor being on the French or Italian or Chinese teams, I cannot grant all requests and still fill all roles. My second reason for refusal is subtler but no less important. As the next section details, the simulation teaches the vital lesson that being on the same team carries no guarantee that goals will be identical or even complementary. The Chinese team begins in a state of near civil war. The Japanese army and navy have radically different objectives. Germany's Himmler wants a solution to the Jewish problem rapidly and regardless of cost. Germany's Schacht wonders if there is a Jewish problem and is certain to balk at any costs involved in any solution.

Rival goals within teams are not unique to my simulation. That apprentice printer in *Stages of Power* can turn a pretty penny by divulging the script to Shakespeare's play, a leak the rest of his company will hardly be happy about. While most members of the suffragist faction in *Greenwich Village* are true believers, some harbor feelings about the importance of organized labor or immigrants that put them at odds with their sisters.

Having "best friends" from real life on the same team in a simulation invites compromising the roles each student is to represent. A student-Himmler might decide to forgo anti-Semitic policies if best friend student-Schacht stands against them, or student-Schacht might decide to go along with the Final Solution rather than risk out-of-class tension or stress. In any such cases, the instructor has to vigilantly remind students that, in class, the role is supreme, even to the extent of reminding students that their simulation grade will suffer otherwise. Once any student believes that she or he can ignore the role, the simulation begins to break down for everyone.

Problems of a related nature can occur whether students know each other out of class or not. Should accommodations be made for, say, the two female students in a class of thirty? The single African American? Should Asian American (or Asian) students be encouraged or discouraged from placement on the Chinese or Japanese teams? Presumably, a shy student would use the role selection mechanic to avoid the role of Hitler, but what if she or he ends up as a Churchill, Roosevelt, or any of a host of roles that might eventually assume real leadership responsibilities?

My answer to these questions is the same one I give to the best friends issue. It is vital to stress to the student, whoever he or she is, whatever their background or outlook, that they are not themselves once they step through the classroom door. They become their character; nothing else should bear on how they conduct themselves. They are not Cory, Cristina, Cassem, or Chiharu any more. They are Chamberlain, Churchill, Halifax, and Eden. They should address each other with their characters' names. They should see simulation events, developments, and decisions as their characters would.

For every student I have known, this exercise is one of discovery and revelation. An Arab American student who played Himmler came to me at semester's end, confessing that he had never understood Jewish sensitivities until he had figuratively put on his SS uniform in the simulation. An African American woman who had rejoiced at the start of class because she was able to be Franklin Roosevelt wrote me after her graduation that she had seen the burdens of the presidency as utterly overwhelming, and lost no opportunity to defend politicians before her friends and students,[9] something she had never dreamed she would be doing. A student athlete who became Léon Blum confessed his complete shock at reading of Blum's near encounter with death by beating at the hands of French anti-Semites. Blum didn't look like much from his photograph, the student said, but he must have been a lot tougher than most people by continuing in office after that. A student who was a perpetual wallflower in my other classes, who himself drew the Roosevelt position, astounded everyone by calling a global summit for peace and giving an impassioned speech asking for an end of hostilities. He was not a wallflower in other classes thereafter.

Special mention is deserved for the role of Winston Churchill, an iconic figure of the era of *Rivalries*. Nearly always, and despite specific course materials indicating otherwise, students grabbing the role of Churchill begin the semester assuming that the prime ministership, and global glory, is their inevitable destiny. They are shocked, to a person, to discover the high walls that the historical Churchill had to climb to earn his statue in Westminster. Churchill endured many lean years, championing causes from warning about the Nazi danger—in which he was proven correct— to championing the maintenance of an empire based on racist assumptions and a monarch who repeatedly showed questionable judgment, in which he would align himself with the not-so-correct. And not-so-popular.

Churchill begins the simulation with the weakest political base among Britain's leaders. He will find it nearly impossible to secure a majority of the British Conservative Party's support, bad news since it was by far the dominant party of these years. Somehow the actual Churchill had to cobble together an interparty coalition, then maintain it while fighting off Nazi Germany and securing foreign support. Student-Churchills, even the most successful ones themselves, end the semester overwhelmed by what their historical counterpart accomplished. If the real Churchill had not pulled it off, they aver, they would have thought his achievements impossible.[10]

Roles in a simulation are terrific learning experiences. They are also great levelers. Students accustomed to lead must learn to negotiate and cooperate. Students inclined to passively observe find it easier to step out and step up once they step into their roles and set aside their own reserve. All these considerations make your definition and preparation of those roles vital to the success of your simulation. Here is how I did mine:

Creating Roles: *Great Power Rivalries* as a Test Case

If you will be using an off-the-shelf simulation, such as any of those available from the Reacting to the Past collection or related ones, you can stop here and proceed to chapter 3. This section will be of primary interest to instructors willing to try their hand at developing their own classroom sims. To that end, I recount how I determined which character, or roles, would appear in my *Great Power Rivalries*.

I am not going to go over all thirty-five roles. You can contact me and I will send you my full character roster.[11] But here I will summarize my reasoning for my selections for four of the eight national teams.

Hitler's Germany: Structuring Roles in a Nazi Dictatorship

I do not write role sheets for each character in my simulation. But I do give the students background information on their nation at the start of the simulation. Doing so not only sets the scene, it also introduces them to each other's characters and explains how they will interact. These interactions are different for each power in *Great Power Rivalries*, hardly surprising because some were dictatorships, others democracies, and still others something else entirely.

Here is my backgrounder for Nazi Germany:

By the start of 1936 (when the simulation begins), Adolf Hitler had eliminated the German socialists and communists from political consideration. He had neutralized the Catholic Church's political influence and had tamed his own SA (Brownshirts). Hitler is a dictator—though not an absolute one. The German business community is an ally, grateful for the end of the Leftist threat but still wary of Hitler's own program, whatever it turns out to be. The German army is pleased over the demise of the SA, which it saw as a possible paramilitary rival, but many of its senior officers continue to regard Hitler as an unstable dilettante, especially in military affairs. It is also concerned about the rising power of the SS, but sees little it can do for the moment and, in any event, sees no one preferable to Hitler in the chancellorship.

Hitler can solely determine Germany's decisions for Policy Options to be played: all military movements, attacks, and strategies; and spending decisions. Hitler may remove (or reinstate) Schacht from office and remove (or reinstate) von Manstein from command. Himmler can never be removed and can never go into "rebellion." Hitler does not control any SS military or the German navy.

Ordinarily, Hess (or, if Hess leaves the simulation, von Ribbentrop) will prepare the Policy Option portion of Germany's turnsheet, Schacht the budget, and von Manstein (and Hess) the army (and navy) orders. NOTE: No points may be spent on building naval points until Policy Option GE-29 is played successfully.

Schacht, one of the Nazi Party's most successful fund raisers and currently the government's Economics Minister, can "dissent" on any or all spending decisions and, as the simulation opens, is having increasing doubts about Hitler's stress on arms spending and, though not in any economic vein, the increasingly obvious Jewish policy of the Nazi Party. If he dissents, Hitler may either follow Schacht's spending decisions or insist upon his own. If he insists, Schacht is removed from office and becomes eligible to initiate his independent rebellion Policy Options (described below) or, he may become, for the purposes of the simulation, Hermann Göring (with possible additional class assignments as a result). So long as Schacht remains, Germany will obtain a small but significant income bonus at starting (that is, low) Production Levels.

Hess acts as Foreign Minister and must sign off on Germany's Policy Options. He may dissent, in which case there is a chance that the Policy Option will not even be attempted the turn in which it is played. In addition, Hess (for the purposes of the simulation—not historically accurate) controls all aspects of Germany's naval assets.

Von Manstein represents the senior officers of the Wehrmacht, the German army. He can dissent on any or all military decisions (move, attack, strategy). Hitler may either concur with von Manstein's dissent or overrule him. If he overrules, von Manstein is removed from office and becomes eligible to initiate his independent rebellion Policy Options (described below). In addition, von Manstein, while Germany is at war with any major power, has complete control over movement, attack, and strategy of the "front" he is appointed to command. A front is defined as a continuous line of connected map sectors in any single map. Von Manstein is a "Gifted Commander." So long as he is "in office" he enjoys the advantages in army combat of that designation.

Himmler controls the SS. As such, he is responsible for ensuring the efficient implementation of Nazi racial policies. It is also possible that the SS will acquire its own military capabilities. In this case, Himmler has absolute control over all aspects of the SS military.

A good simulation design does not simply aim for verisimilitude; it must attempt to re-create dynamics among its participants allowing for a variety of alternative yet plausible outcomes. The design sets the stage. The student actors play things out, without a fixed script but within the bounds of the world being re-created. Those bounds, whatever they are, must allow for each role—each student—to make decisions that are interesting and that can affect the simulation overall.

For Nazi Germany, doing so presents a challenge at the outset. Hitler begins *Rivalries* in an exceptionally powerful position. His role in the simulation should re-create that power, but it should also allow for restrictions on it and, under appropriate circumstances, challenges to it. A well-designed German team should also incorporate student roles that will remind Hitler what his role is and what he needs to achieve to be a successful Nazi.[12]

The primary "supporting" or reinforcing role falls to Heinrich Himmler, historically head of the SS. Students assigned to be Himmler quickly get the idea that their SS should get considerable resources, even at the expense of the German army. Himmlers will, if properly played, constantly remind their German counterparts of the need to move eastward in order to best position their *blackshirts* for anti-Jewish operations.

There are no true opposition roles in Nazi Germany. But just as Hitler was not an absolute dictator, the simulation's Germany should allow for other centers of power. I chose to incorporate two such centers: the German army, represented by Erich von Manstein, and the German financial community, represented by Hjalmar Schacht.

In a sense, even actual historical characters are composite ones. I could have selected any number of senior generals to represent the German army. In fact, I could have chosen two or three or more such generals, if I wanted a larger German team. Why von Manstein? In part, I used the process of elimination. Wilhelm Keitel was widely seen, and despised, by his fellow officers as Hitler's yes-man. Student-Keitels would have little to do beyond writing army orders. Heinz Guderian, a brilliant field commander, showed considerable courage is disputing Hitler's decisions and priorities, especially military ones, but he held no strong political views and was in no position to act on any if he had, as his irascible, nearly arrogant personality alienated many fellow generals. Claus von Stauffenberg, point man of the attempt to assassinate Hitler in 1944, is too junior, but he did have support from more senior officers such as Henning von Tresckow and, at times, Gunther von Klüge.

None of these seem quite right. To settle on either Keitel or von Tresckow straitjackets the student. Von Manstein was not only in between these positions, he actively sought to obfuscate his own position, making for an interesting research task for the student representing him. Von Manstein was widely respected as an able, even gifted, commander. But his critics will point to his testimony at the postwar trial at Nuremberg, noting how he was one of the authors of the "clean hands" myth—that the German army was uninvolved with, or at least did not intentionally collaborate in, the various and horrific war crimes of the Nazi era, from brutal treatment of Soviet prisoners of war to the Final Solution. Von Manstein argued that the German army was an apolitical institution that simply fulfilled its mission of applying armed force to the enemies of the nation it served. For me, these arguments are powerful ones for picking von Manstein in the first place. No diligent student representing von

Manstein will fail to discover that his army was quite dirty indeed. Really good students will ferret out the truth: that von Manstein was adept at distorting the historical record and disguising his role in such activities.

The chief problem in using von Manstein in the simulation is not his deviousness, but his belief that the army should remain out of politics no matter what. "Field marshals do not mutiny," he is reported to have said. Time and again, when Germany (due to Hitler) has plunged into disaster, and the student-Schacht tries to enlist the army's help against the Nazis, a distressed student von Manstein will come to me and argue that while they personally would like nothing better than ousting the Nazis, doing so would be contrary to being their character.

Choosing a different German army officer, one that did join, or at least sympathize with, one of the various assassination or other attempts against Hitler historically, would surmount this problem. Von Klüge would be one possibility, as he was far more open to getting rid of the Nazis. But choosing him raises two problems of its own. Von Manstein might have distorted his own record; but that record, and historians' assessments of it, are readily available and in English. Von Klüge gives the student much less to work with. In addition, the stark fact is that von Manstein was more typical of senior German officers than von Klüge, coming from a generation that had lived through the catastrophe of the First World War and its immediate aftermath, upheavals that convinced many officers of that generation that far more harm came from mixing into politics than following the wishes of whoever controlled the wider apparatus of the state. In my view, von Manstein better epitomizes the perspective of most senior officers in the German army, so he gets the role.

The other non-Nazi center of power is represented by Schacht. Schacht, like many German conservative elites, played a vital part in the Nazis' rise to power. Schacht himself served in Hitler's government until he resigned his position as Economics Minister in 1937. A strong believer in German nationalism, he had thought that Hitler represented the best way to recover full German sovereignty, which had been hobbled under the Versailles Treaty ending the First World War. This recovery was certainly achieved, but Schacht had increasing misgivings about Hitler's rush toward a new war and was repulsed by the Nazis' increasingly strident anti-Semitism. Hitler was aware of the Nazis' image abroad as a set of low-class demagogues and thugs, and insisted that the refined and internationally respected Schacht remain in the government even after his resignation, but the vague definition of powers of Schacht's new post, and his day-to-day clashes with his replacement, Hermann Göring, compelled Hitler to dismiss him entirely in 1943, by which time international impressions mattered rather less. After elements in the German army attempted Hitler's assassination and a coup against the Nazi regime a year later, Schacht was arrested by the SS on suspicion of plotting with the German resistance to Hitler and sent to a concentration camp. He was freed by US troops just before the end of the war in Europe and put on trial by the victors at Nuremberg, where he was acquitted of charges largely as a result of Britain's argument that, though misguided at first, Schacht had not been party to Germany's war of aggression and the violations of human rights that had accompanied it. With dry wit, he then penned memoirs entitled *My First Seventy-Six Years*.

This brief biography makes clear Schacht's value for the simulation. The challenge is how to incorporate Schacht's changing perspective, his abilities, and his fate into a role that a student will find engaging through the entire semester. Historically, Schacht was a banking wizard who provided indispensable financial support for the Nazis until his resignation. In the simulation, he has a special Policy Option allowing him to boost German national income. This boost is modest and fixed, but it provides a high percentage increase for the early part of the simulation. Schacht can withdraw it at any time, and in most simulations does so as soon as Germany either goes to war against another major power or begins active persecution of its Jewish population.

So far, so good. Schacht has leverage. But what happens after he loses it by withdrawing his contribution to German national income? Prospects for the rest of the semester look unappealing for the student representing him (as they did for the real Schacht from 1937 to 1943). Students in past simulations, told by the instructor that they needed to find their own way, have found three. The first follows Schacht's historical path. Anxiously wait while remaining on the German team, hoping that reason will return either from within Germany or, more likely, from outside. The second seizes on some historical evidence suggesting that Schacht did more than contact the German Resistance but actually participated in it. Students taking this path usually try to cultivate the German army, a foreign power (usually Britain), or both. In cases where the Nazi regime falls, student-Schachts who took this course are well positioned to become the new masters of Germany, and a fair number have done just that in prior simulations.

The third way is to abandon the Schacht character altogether and become, as the Team Rules of Play above allow, Hermann Göring, returning to the office of Economics Minister in Göring's shoes. In this case, Göring gets his own, quite modest, boost to German national income, which he may spend as he pleases. (Göring was notorious for many things, the notoriety here centers on his proclivity to skim for his own benefit.) If the student representing Schacht makes this switch, he has to write a role sheet for Göring, so the transition is not entirely painless. But if the student is confident of a Nazi victory, Göring becomes an attractive option. If that guess about victory turns out to be wrong, well, a look at Göring's actual end provides a resolution.

The final member of the German team is a bit of a wild card. Rudolf Hess, at one time second to Hitler himself in the Nazi Party, must rank as one of the least studied of one of the most studied leadership groups in the history of humankind. His bizarre, ill-fated solo flight to Scotland in May 1941, seeking peace between Germany and Britain, has both engaged the enduring interests of conspiracy theorists[13] and contributed to most professional historians giving Hess a wide berth. To further complicate things, Hess has become a cult figure of the hard right in today's Germany. Isn't this a real challenge to any student researching Hess, not to mention an invitation to undergraduate role-playing mischief? Why even consider a role for Hess in *Great Power Rivalries*?

Part of the answer is to provide a vital limitation to what a student-Hitler can do in the simulation. Whatever else he was, Hess was a devoted Nazi, fastidious in his attention to the details of its ideology, beliefs, and protocols. His flight to Scotland, just weeks before Germany attacked the Soviet Union, was propelled by his conviction that the British, as brother "Aryans," would follow their blood, end their resistance against Germany, and join in the war against the reds. For student-Hitlers more inclined to be Machiavellis, the roles of Hess and Himmler will provide guidance and, if necessary, correction.

But the role of Hess holds a key difference, one that reinforces the desirability of including Hess in the simulation. Himmler was loyal to Hitler. Hess was loyal to Nazi ideals. Hess could—and historically did—defy

Hitler in a way Himmler could not. Hess' flight to Scotland triggered a full-blown crisis within the Nazi Party.[14] It also emboldened critics of that party, who attributed Germany's immense wartime success up to that date to the German army and its conservative supporters. Students of the Third Reich rarely get to see this side of it. Having Hess as a character on the German team allows them to do so.

But if Hess is on the German team, and if Hess has an option to fly to Britain, what happens to him if—as occurred historically—the British politely decline his offer to make peace with Germany and join it against the Soviet Union? Historically, Hess had the signal dishonor of being the first Nazi leader incarcerated by a wartime opponent.[15] Few students in the role of Hess will be likely to undertake such a risk knowing that the remainder of their semester will be spent in a figurative jail.[16]

Other simulation roles call for similar consideration. Among the first questions that students assigned to France invariably ask is: what happens after France is conquered? I will turn to France shortly. For the student-Hess, though, the only satisfactory solution, once Hess' options are gone, is to become another character altogether. In *Rivalries*, that character has been Joachim von Ribbentrop. Ribbentrop was historically Nazi Germany's foreign minister. He was not terribly distinguished in real life. But his character plays an important role in the dynamics of the simulation.

Great Power Rivalries physically isolates its students by national teams.[17] Fascist Germany, Italy, and Japan locate in one room. Democracies Britain, France, and the United States stay in another. The Soviet Union and China have their own, independent spaces.

Besides the obvious need for confidentiality from one's likely foes, this isolation gives significance to interteam negotiations, otherwise known as diplomacy. If heads of state could freely travel to other rooms, they would do so, cutting their teammates out of the diplomatic loop. That is bad for the other students. It is also ahistorical. Summit conferences were exceptionally rare in the 1930s. Hitler needs a diplomat and Hitler needs to see that his top diplomat does not have ulterior motives. Historically, Hitler distrusted the German Foreign Ministry, fearing it did not share his goals for Germany. Even those professional diplomats who did, like Konstantin von Neurath—whom Ribbentrop replaced—questioned Hitler's eagerness for war, an attitude Hitler could not tolerate. Having Neurath instead of Ribbentrop as Hitler's Foreign Minister will tempt the student playing

Hitler either to become his own foreign minister and leave the student-Neurath in the cold, not optimal in a semester-long course, or to do as the real Hitler did and fire Neurath, replacing him with Ribbentrop, a request that would be difficult to deny. To be sure, a Neurath imposed on the German team could serve as a break on Hitler's (and Himmler's) ambitions, but the roles of von Manstein and Schacht already have something of that function within their portfolios.

Germany needs a conduit to other teams in the simulation. Hess can play such a role at the simulation's start. He begins as someone with Hitler's trust. Hess, though historically preoccupied with Nazi Party affairs, clearly had an interest in Germany's place in the world. In several respects, Hess is a perfect prequel to Ribbentrop, as well as a neat solution to having a student-Neurath walking on eggs until student-Hitler finally decides to drop the hammer.

But what if a national team has no one with a hammer? No clearly defined leadership roles? For that matter, no clearly defined leader?

France: The Structural Difficulties of Democracies

There was no Hitler in France, so there is no Hitler-type role for the French team. The criteria for choosing roles for France is radically different as a result. Who gets to sit at the French table—and who gets to sit as leader of that table—makes for difficult simulation design decisions, not least because the ways these roles interact must be within the simulated dynamics of a democracy.

Democracies require the simulation to model two key features: (1) elections, to decide who holds which office, and (2) parliamentary voting, to decide budgetary and other policy decisions. The simulation requires considerable simplification of both, but their essences must be retained. To use France as a case study: parliament will not be bicameral, as students would have to manipulate their votes in both houses, a needless complication. The number of historical parties in both the legislature and at the polls has to be reduced, as France had over a dozen major party blocs in the 1930s.

Even so, France—and Britain and the United States—will have larger teams, not only to reflect the various political blocs and constituencies that democracies have, but also to complicate and slow internal decision-making in comparison to the dictatorships. For France, this larger team is both blessing and curse. Blessing, because a broad array of those blocs can be represented. Curse, because not all can be. Some important historical characters are going to be left out, a factor that makes the instructor's choice of characters all the more important.

Again it becomes tempting to streamline things by inventing hypothetical, composite characters and writing their role sheets yourself. But if one of your objectives in running the simulation is to acquaint your students with research skills as well as their characters, this temptation should be resisted. For Britain and the United States, learning to research historical characters is simple. English-language scholarship abounds. For France, any policy maker selected should have at least a toehold of such scholarship, another element playing into choice of characters.

There may be no French Hitler, Mussolini, or Stalin—no indispensable single policy maker. But there are perspectives and personalities that merit consideration. The first is Maurice Thorez.

Thorez led the French Communist Party during the period of *Great Power Rivalries*. He never became prime minister. He fled conscription into the French army in 1939 and was tried and sentenced to death while in exile in the Soviet Union. He returned to France five years later. His citizenship was restored and his party became the largest immediately after Germany's surrender. He refused to destabilize the reconstituted French Fourth Republic and became vice-premier from 1946 to 1947, until the growing Cold War between the United States and Soviet Union led to the withdrawal of French communists from the French government.

There is appallingly little English-language scholarship on Thorez. Even so, he is an indispensable member of the French team. His party played a vital role in France's ability or failure to form left-wing coalitions, or "Popular Fronts," both before and after World War II. As a communist, meaning a communist loyal to Stalin, Thorez' presence on the French team startlingly affects its interstudent dynamics. Student-Thorez, for example, can hinder French income by unilaterally calling for strikes or demonstrations. But the biggest effect comes through a simple device of the simulation: the ability to leave the room.

Recall the restrictions on student movement. Hitler and Mussolini must remain in the fascist room. Stalin must stay in a Soviet-only room. All three can send their foreign ministers (or any other student) to another room for discussion and negotiation, but only with the instructor's permission. No student, from any team, can leave their room without that permission—except two. Chinese communist leader Mao Zedong can visit the Soviet room freely. So can Thorez.

Here too the simulation has engaged in design-for-effect. The actual Mao had no jet service to Moscow; the real Thorez no hot line to Stalin. But student-Thorez' ability to consult with Stalin at will, then return to "Paris" in the democracy room, creates instant suspicion among the rest of the French team (and, for that matter, the British and US characters who share that room). Whom is Thorez loyal to? Whose interests does he serve?

These very questions drive the student representing Thorez to do a good deal of research about him, the French Communist Party, and communism in general. They also, whether the student realizes it or not, make her or him a potentially pivotal character in the simulation. Thorez can quell suspicions of the communists among the Western democracies, or he can stimulate those suspicions. Clever Nazis will try to drive Thorez to do the latter, playing up the "real" danger to the West of communism. Clever Stalins will urge the former, unless of course the simulation reproduces the historical Nazi-Soviet nonaggression pact. In any case, Thorez must be on the French team. As must Léon Blum.

Léon Blum led the French Socialist Party and, for a time, the Popular Front coalition government. Student-Blums have been fascinated by his career. He was the first Jewish premier of France. He was beaten nearly to death by rightists shortly before assuming that office. He championed a wave of labor reforms, and was the first to give women cabinet positions, yet he refused to aid the Spanish socialists and communists once civil war against the army and fascists broke out there in 1936. In the simulation, student-Blum faces a constant question of how to relate to Thorez and the communists, just as the actual Blum did in reality. There are number of book-length studies on Blum in English, one quite recent. Blum is always a safe and interesting role. As is Édouard Daladier.

Daladier headed the Radical Party which was anything but. The Radicals in fact were a centrist party. Daladier was France's premier during such key events as the Czech Crisis of 1938, which led to the Munich Agreement, and France's declaration of war against Germany a year later. Daladier had no love for communism. Some of his key domestic measures rolled back those of the communist-socialist Popular Front under Blum, especially regarding labor rights. But he remained certain that Hitler was France's chief threat and spearheaded a dedicated rearmament effort toward that end. While Pierre Laval is French premier at the start of the simulation in 1936, Daladier often becomes prime minister for the majority of the semester. The reason? France is a parliamentary democracy, and this type of democracy tends toward party coalitions including the center. The role of Daladier fills the middle.

Filling the French Right is more problematic. There were ultraright organizations in France, but none cast up leaders with the heft of Blum or large following of Thorez. More fundamentally, there are no major leaders who were consistently right of Daladier throughout this period. The closest might be Pierre Laval.

Laval has the distinction of having been France's leader under both the Third Republic and the Nazi occupation. He ranks as one of the most despised French figures of all time for his years of collaboration, years he defended vigorously though unsuccessfully at his postwar trial for treason. For these reasons, there are mountains of scholarship on Laval, though much of it remained heavily influenced by deep political divides in postwar France.

Some students will be entranced by these divides and see Laval as a champion of the French Right, a dedicated foe of communism even to the extent of opposing war against the Nazis. This misreads history. Laval, like most of his compatriots, dreaded such a war, but much of his prewar diplomacy focused on avoiding it through the creation of anti-German alliances and strong French rearmament. Only after France's fall did he elect to remain in country, bargain (controversially) for the Nazis' release of French prisoners of war and (even more controversially) agree to help form what amounted to a collaborationist government.

Whether student-Lavals hew to the simple or more nuanced version of the actual man, they will represent historically accurate constituencies and, not least, present intriguing options for France overall, especially if France does fall. The actual Laval, like most in France, believed that the war was over after that fall. That Germany had won it. That there was dawning a new order for all Europe. In the simulation, these possibilities are real. Laval, in its world, might find his choices vindicated.

France could stand pat with roles for Thorez, Blum, Daladier, and Laval. But doing so virtually cedes the prime ministership to Daladier unless Thorez and Blum can pull off and prolong their sometimes awkward, always fragile historical alliance. Daladier had rivals in the political center, such as Paul Reynaud. And there were French leaders who, unlike all the above, were unabashed proponents of any measure of appeasement that avoided a new war against Germany. Georges Bonnet was among the most influential proponent of this view. After many experiments of a French team with one or the other, I have concluded that, if student enrollment allows, I should have both. A team of six is big and sure to be unwieldy, just like France's Third Republic.

The United States: The Struggle against Boredom

If you are running a simulation like *Trial of Galileo*, there is always a center stage and all the students' attention will focus on it. There will be several such centers in *Greenwich Village*, but all activity aims at winning the final session's vote. But in *Great Power Rivalries*, the action is more diffuse. This diffusion is especially evident within the team of students representing the United States, a nation which often goes through the simulation and semester without entering any war or even any alliance. There is nothing historically inaccurate about that state of affairs, or lack thereof. But it can make for the bane of any simulation—students with nothing to do. As bad, President Franklin Roosevelt was a towering figure in this period historically. He was not a dictator, but he wielded enormous influence, especially over US foreign policy. It is possible but unlikely that any other US character will replace him in the White House.

The possible lack of any activities abroad and the dominance of Roosevelt at home has led some of my former students, who have taken to running their own *Great Power Rivalries* for simulation alumni, to omit US roles altogether. There is too great a chance that the United States, and the students on the US team, will have no interesting options from one turn to the next.

For a game, leaving out the United States is possible. For a simulation of great power rivalries from 1936 to 1947, it is not. As history shows, it is possible for the United States to become deeply involved in world affairs (and world wars) in these years and that involvement can become decisive. There has to be a US team. I provide five US roles, realizing that I am going to have to devise things for each of them to do that are both engaging in the simulation and historically accurate. That the United States of that era was a democracy turns out to make both possible.

The United States is a presidential, not parliamentary, democracy, a fact that at once cements Roosevelt's powerful control over decisions from the start of the simulation until at least the presidential elections of 1940.[18] Yet he still will need support from allies, especially for some of the bolder Policy Options available to the US team. That means he will need something to offer them in exchange. In days past, this process was referred to as "horse trading" and *Great Power Rivalries* aims to replicate it within the US team.

Horse trading, though, means different aims for each member of that team. Each has to have different priorities so that mutually beneficial bargains can be made. To that end, history (and lifetimes of characters) need to be tweaked a bit. But, as with France, the object is to create roles that will interact in historically plausible ways. Two Republicans, a Democrat, and a "betweener" will join the US team.

Robert Taft and Richard Russell are obvious choices. Taft was rightly termed "Mr. Republican" and, upon his election to the Senate in 1938, became leader of his party and a bipartisan coalition opposed to Roosevelt. His steadfast opposition to deep involvement in the developing European conflict saw him smeared as an isolationist and hindered his quest for the Republican presidential nomination in 1940. He would be frustrated then and thereafter by more moderate Republicans through 1952, when he lost to Dwight Eisenhower. He died a year later.

Russell was a conservative too, but a southern Democrat. A dedicated foe of any racial or civil rights reform, he, like most of his southern colleagues, was inclined to bless Roosevelt's efforts to aid the other Western democracies. He was particularly anti-Japanese and, after Pearl Harbor, would advocate the strongest possible measures against them.

It would be no crime to stop with these three for the US team. But doing so hands the Republican nomination to Taft and it leaves little room for complex horse trades. So I have customarily added two more characters: Wendell Willkie and Hiram Johnson.

Hiram who? Any Californian a century ago could have answered. Johnson entered politics after his successful prosecution of corruption in San Francisco, becoming one of the longest serving US senators in the history of that state. He was a leader of the progressive wing of the Republican

Party, quite different from Taft. He was also a dedicated opponent of US entanglements abroad and a powerful foe of membership in the League of Nations. Favorably inclined to Roosevelt's domestic New Deal reforms, Johnson moved into opposition later in the 1930s, especially over Roosevelt's steps toward involvement in foreign crises.

Willkie also entered politics through his legal career, but otherwise had little in common with Johnson. His clients included private utility corporations in the Midwest. Initially active as a Democrat, Willkie strongly opposed one of Roosevelt's key domestic programs: the establishment of a government-owned Tennessee Valley Authority (TVA) that would offer cheap electricity in the region. Willkie made a name for himself in a dogged, though ultimately failed, fight against the TVA. But his chief claim to fame, and to membership on the US team in the simulation, came when he received the Republican nomination for president in 1940. Willkie, who had joined the party only a year before, got it as the only prominent candidate to agree with Roosevelt's foreign policy, especially active US assistance to Britain and France.

Including Johnson and Willkie results in a well-balanced ring of five, each with differing priorities and perspectives. Just as vitally, it will be clear to each student where her or his character might stand on the issues and decisions encountered in the simulation. For Roosevelt's domestic programs, he can rely on Johnson (and sometimes Russell) for support, while Taft (and sometimes Russell and Willkie) will oppose. For his foreign policy, Roosevelt can count on Russell and Willkie, but will have to contend with Taft and Johnson.

For the desired horse trading to take place, the US team is going to need a robust menu of Policy Options that will interest its various characters, much more detailed than for any other team in the simulation. For *Great Power Rivalries*, I introduced quite a few of these. They include National Health Insurance, Public Electricity for All, Anti-Lynching legislation, Farm Price Supports, relaxation of immigration laws, enlarging the Supreme Court, and even a federal school lunch program, among others. Students are encouraged to use their own research into their own characters to propose other Options.

Many of these Options are of the "over my dead body" sort. Russell will oppose anti-lynching vigorously, Willkie any move to expand public electricity. Some will appeal to most characters, though Taft will have reservations about free lunches for school kids. The objective is to foster horse trading and, to be frank, keep the US team busy until foreign crises and war overwhelms them, if ever. My efforts appear to have succeeded. Students in past simulations, especially on the British and French teams, have loudly criticized US self-centeredness, and the US presidential contests (which themselves are a simulation within the simulation) have become a spectator sport for everyone. In a majority of simulations, the United States does not go to war against anyone, but the students on the US team have plenty to do.

China: The Struggle of All against All

China of the 1930s is neither democracy nor dictatorship and the Chinese team in *Great Power Rivalries* is not a team. China is a divided country that will ultimately see a civil war between the nationalists of Jiang Jieshi (Chiang Kai-shek)[19] and communists under Mao Zedong (Mao Tse-tung).

These two roles are necessary. But I have found it almost as vital to include a third: Wang Jingwei (Wang Ching-wei). Whereas Mao Zedong and Jiang Jieshi are well-known figures, both subjects of voluminous scholarship even in English, Wang is unheard of and has little written about him. He was a leading figure in the Nationalist Party until the late 1920s, when Jiang eclipsed him. He remained at odds with Jiang thereafter, finally making an open break against him in 1940. In that year, Wang agreed to head a rival Chinese government in collaboration with the Japanese and based in Japanese-occupied China. He died in 1944, receiving treatment in Japan for a failed assassination attempt against him. He was reviled as a traitor by both nationalists and communists, quite a feat!

Students who draw Wang as their character often despair as they begin researching him. He has virtually no resources to draw on and no support inside or outside China. It is like being assigned a French character after France has already fallen. What are they supposed to do?

They are supposed to do what every other student does: study the character they are playing. Once they do so, they begin to grasp Wang's options and role. He is a necessary third wheel. Wang gives Jiang limits, opening possibilities for both himself and Mao. Jiang is perfectly free to pursue an understanding with Japan, but doing so might hand Wang enough clout, or political influence, to win control of the nationalists. This possibility might make the Japanese think twice before approaching Jiang themselves. Or it might make Wang a better Chinese partner for them, certainly a possibility drawn from real history. Wang can force Jiang to behave like a nationalist, in other words, complicating his efforts to crush Mao. Finally, having Wang in play, as a third member and third force on the Chinese team, makes cultivating the support of regional warlords more important and more intense.

As with France and the United States, so also for China: the instructor's selection of individual character roles has to be made with an eye toward how those roles will interact with each other within a national team. Roles are the bedrock of any simulation. If they are carelessly chosen the entire structure will be rickety.

But roles are only the foundation. Once their casting has been completed, the actors have to be given something meaningful to do once the simulation begins. Because a simulation is not a reenactment, because it is not a play with a script, it needs a structure—a set of rules of play—that will at once allow room for students to make choices that affect their team or the entire class, but do so in a way that ensures they remain acting within their roles. One of the most crucial issues in many simulations arises from how to deal with roles that many or all of your students find highly offensive.

Nazis in the Classroom

Our identities are defined by what offends us. Abortion opponents cannot get the image of a screaming fetus out of their heads. Immigration advocates are appalled by children kept in cages. Bigots can't stand the sight or smell of a person of a different skin color or eye shape, or someone who can't or won't speak their language, or who might simply have a regional accent. Some cringe at men holding hands or kissing in public. A century ago, it was unthinkable that a Catholic could run for the US presidency: many saw the Democratic Party standing for Rum, Romanism, and Rebellion, and most Democrats as drunks and traitors. Antebellum Southerners were appalled to see Blacks free; abolitionists by the sight of them in chains. Mohammad Atta of 9/11 infamy wrote a postgraduate thesis decrying Western architecture that, to him, destroyed cityscapes, neighborhoods, and families with its skyscrapers' obscene grasp for the heavens. His actions that day would lead others to see the minarets of Islam as nests of devils.

There are plenty of triggers out there, things that we would prefer not to exist, or at least not to see or hear. But one trigger has trumped them all for nearly a century now: Nazism. The visceral, guttural hatreds that Nazism fostered, and the actions they carried out using the power of one of the strongest nations on earth, has ensured that symbols like the swastika and expressions of anti-Semitism have remained at the top of the totem pole of offend and appall.

Teaching about things like Nazism, slavery, nativism, and prejudice is essential unless the past is to be ignored altogether. But there are various ways to dilute the disgust. The lecturer can make clear that the excerpts of Nazi speeches are just that, and not her own words or feelings. Or she can just skip Nazi rhetoric altogether. Slavery can be discussed as an economic system, with its human tragedy and pain left to the imagination. Anti-Catholic hatred can be presented in a "Can you believe it?" sort of way, with pats on the back that humanity has progressed since the medieval times of the 1920s.

These options are not open in a simulation that includes such third-rail components, especially Nazism. How should students cast as Nazis behave in the classroom? How should they be regarded by other students in the simulation?

For me, as this chapter should make clear, an effective simulation requires authentic roles. All students should be able to freely and fully embrace their roles within the confines of the simulation and its physical space. But: totally freely and totally fully? Even the students with Nazi roles?

The ideal answer is *yes*. Few things drive student engagement with their subjects more than role-playing them.[20] My student-Maos fairly beam with pride when they stride in in their CCP jackets and caps. Red shirts became the dress of the day among many Soviet team members, and one team brought a bust of Stalin to every class to reinforce just who was in charge. Several Neville Chamberlains took to carrying umbrellas about. Churchills would sport cigars, thankfully unlit. There were the inevitable berets and trench coats among the French team. The Japanese corner of their room boasted the Rising Sun flag, and several students there donned *hachimakis*.[21]

But, with two exceptions, the students on my German teams never donned Nazi regalia. They never wrote Nazi slogans on the board in their room (the Japanese often did, and sometimes the Italians). They never delivered public speeches reflecting Nazi ideology.[22]

So, should we put our trust in the students' good sense of where the bounds of offense are? Not entirely, perhaps, but a simulation can be structured not to tempt such crossings. For example, *Rivalries* requires discussions, negotiations, and decisions. But it does not require speech-making, as quite a few other simulations do. No one has to deliver a hate-laced tirade. Even if they did, it would reach a limited audience, as only Japan and Italy share the same room as the German team.[23] For a student inclined to mischief or malice, there would be little incentive to imitate Nazi propaganda minister Goebbels.

To be sure, *Rivalries* does require that Germany act upon the Nazis' hate. There is a wide range of Policy Options that the German team almost certainly will adopt: a state boycott of Jewish businesses, state confiscation of Jewish assets, expulsion of Jews from Germany, state-sponsored violence against Jews (Kristallnacht), right through the Final Solution. These policies do not require speechmaking, but they are announced in the simulation's newsletter, and often will draw sharp responses from other national teams. Put another way, students on the German team will be called on (or called out) by other students to justify their anti-Semitic actions.

This sort of calling out can become quite dramatic. Several runs of *Rivalries*, in which Germany was conquered as it was historically, saw their own version of the Nuremberg trials to determine the fate of the surviving German characters.[24] Invariably the student prosecutors will emphasize the inhumanity and stark racism of the Nazis, demanding that their actions receive the strongest possible punishments.

Just as invariably, the student-Nazis refuse to back down. They will ask how many other nations were free of anti-Semitism. They will argue that their actions pale in comparison to Britain's record of racism and bloodletting in Africa or South Asia, or the United States' in North America. (Students on the Japanese and Chinese teams will often silently nod on these points.) They will point to Stalin's slaughter of his own people by the millions, and his regime's sponsorship of global communist revolution, often through violence.[25]

These attacks customarily get weak responses, noting that Nazi Germany is on trial, not the West or the USSR, to which good student-Nazis snort, "the victors write the history." It is a fine teachable moment. Every student at the trial will sit back and rethink what they have been learning about these years—including my assignments and lectures.

To bring us full circle, they will also consider why Nazism remains so offensive to this day. It is hard to have this sort of conversation if the simulation restricts thinking about what the Third Reich said and did.

Even so, the fact remains that while the class may allow communist denunciations of capitalism and imperialism, or the wearing of red shirts or caps with red stars. While it might tolerate the most naked expressions of Japanese expansionist rhetoric. Still, if it permits open expression of Nazi ideals or open display of Nazi symbols, there is likely to be trouble for the students and instructor alike. As a recent keynote speaker at a Reacting conference noted,[26] the words of an old childhood saying have changed radically, to "Sticks and stones may break my bones, but words can *really* hurt me." A simulation can be structured to limit opportunities to use such words, but how can an instructor be sure that a student will not show up deliberately intending mischief or malice?

The stark fact is that you cannot be sure. You can try to prebuild firewalls, as Robert Goodrich does in his *Democracy in Crisis: Germany, 1929–1932*. Goodrich bans racist and ethnic slurs, Nazis symbols and dress, and the use of expressions such as the "Sieg heil!" and Nazi salute. He stresses that his simulation re-creates the competition of ideas and ideologies, whereas the use of certain words or symbols is purely emotional, deliberately meant to punch the gut. He insists that students respect other students in the simulation as other students, regardless of their roles. Mark Higbee and James Brewer Stewart have similar injunctions in their *Frederick Douglass, Slavery, and the Constitution, 1845*. As Goodrich says, "We can expect discomfort when confronting atrocity, but drawing the line between comfort and true suffering that prevents learning, while not always easy, is what we, as a class, will undertake together."[27]

Drawing that line is not always easy.[28] As the years in the United States since the 2016 presidential campaign should make clear, an important component of political discourse is emotional, deliberately so. This component channels hatred of people deemed outsiders. It flourishes in the soil of tribal solidarity. It rejoices in brutality. Nazism was the most successful expression, so far, of this component. It is essential that students realize that this is the quality that renders Nazism so repugnant. It is perhaps as essential that they realize the world outside the halls of ivory is fairly awash with emotional politics.[29]

These realizations do not require that students wear Nazi costumes, mouth Nazi slogans, or ape Nazi gestures. By the same token, they ought to persuade any student to avoid all of them without the need for explicit prohibition—and to remind other students that their national narratives include a dose of brutal tribalism as well.

As instructor, or simulation designer, you are faced with three broad options. The first is to avoid distressing subjects like slavery or Nazism entirely.[30] The second is to address such subjects but define borders that student behavior, even (or especially) in-character, cannot cross. The third is to trust your students to learn why such borders exist today from their participation in the simulation itself. I'm comfortable with my choice. Be sure you are with yours.

Related questions must be raised for the opposite situation. Perhaps you do not have any malicious students eager to strut their swastikas in class, but have some who do not want to have anything to do with Nazi Germany, or slaveowners, or other offensive characters. Perhaps they have bad personal memories of being targeted as "others," or they had family members or close friends who were. They want nothing to do with any simulation that might unbury such memories or experiences.

In the case of my *Rivalries*, an elective course and a simulation—with Nazis—that runs the entire semester, a student raising such reservations should have a frank conversation with the instructor. If the reservations are high enough, the student should not take the course. In the real world, all too unhappily, real people appalled by Nazism still had to confront it in one form or another. An insulating envelope was impossible virtually anywhere on earth. It certainly would be impossible in *Rivalries*.

But if the simulation is only a part of a course, or part of a required course or high school class, the calculations should be different. It is one thing to hear about Nazi or antebellum ideas about racial differences and hierarchies in a lecture or read about them in a book, quite another to have to meet (or even be) role-players of actual Nazis or white-supremacist slaveholders. In these cases, role assignments dictated by the instructor are a bad idea. It is possible that a student will not want to participate in any role. A conversation about the distance between role and real might be helpful, but if the student is a conscientious objector, some alternative assignment ought to be found.[31]

3

Rules

Rules fulfill two central functions in any classroom simulation. They tell students what they are allowed to do from class to class. And they tell students what they need to do in order to win the simulation. Simulations do not have to feature wars, but they do need competition and victory conditions. Competition and victory give purpose; they also drive student motivation.

Let's take a second look at the three examples—none of them featuring simulated armed conflict—and how they use rules to inform and induce student activities. Then an examination of *Great Power Rivalries*, which does the same thing, but uses different rules for different students.

Greenwich Village: Using Rules to Reinforce Roles

Greenwich Village seeks to immerse its students in what life was like for women, workers, and Bohemians over a century ago. It uses its victory conditions to insist on such immersion. Those conditions are quite simple. During its eighth and final class session, villagers will vote to either join women suffragists who will march the day before Woodrow Wilson's presidential inauguration parade to steal Wilson's thunder and make a show of force for women's demands, or they will go to Madison Square Garden in New York to demonstrate for the Industrial Workers of the World (IWW) and their right to go on strike.

But, just as women begin the simulation without the right to vote, so all students lack that right. They cannot participate in the final class until they have earned their right to vote in it by earning Personal Influence Points, fifteen of them to be exact. The only way to earn these points is by engaging in an in-class activity appropriate to the student's role. The rules reinforce the roles.

A suffragist could earn a point by dressing the part: in bright yellow and white. Or by designing and wearing a hat, button, or poster in support of the cause. Suffragists could stand vigil outside Polly's place. More points can be earned by more involved actions: drawing a suffragist cartoon or performing a skit, writing lyrics to the tune of a suffragist song. Even more are possible from designing a parade float, giving a formal address or, naturally, designing a suffragist game.

Union workers have similar options for earning enough points for the final class vote. Put on an IWW T-shirt, lead the class, or at least a portion of it, in a workers' song, instruct fellow students on how to picket at a strike site, give a pro-union speech—in as many languages of the workers as you can (Yiddish and Italian for the most points), organize a picket yourself, or a study group on the ideas of Marx.

Greenwich Village rules also encourage specific student interactions. Mabel Dodge runs Polly's, a renowned meeting space. If she invites you to give a show and likes it, your points soar. Max Eastman wants to put out a magazine and is looking for exciting material for it. Publication gives points. Emma Goldman can single-handedly tip the final vote—if she has been carefully cultivated by a faction beforehand. If you are a student in *Greenwich Village*, you have a clear idea of what you need to do and how you need to do it from beginning to end of the simulation. In doing so, you are driven to reinforce your role and the roles of the other students you interact with.

Galileo: Mastering Stars and the Cross

The Trial of Galileo establishes rules that likewise drive the students toward immersion in their roles. But it does so with quite different mechanisms. Early class sessions are devoted to ensuring mastery of the (seventeenth-century) state of knowledge in astronomy, mathematics, and church doctrine—with quizzes ensuring that such mastery is adequate for understanding whichever role a student might have. Subsequent sessions feature organized debates with presentations and cross-examinations. The simulation culminates in a vote among church players as to how to advise the pope on Galileo's writings and future. At least one additional class session considers the simulation's course and outcome, serving as a postmortem.

Galileo at first glance appears to be much more structured than Greenwich Village with little student dress-up or spontaneity. While period costumes are not banned, they are not central to creating the you-are-there essence of a simulation. Galileo stresses the importance of grasping the core issues of scientific inquiry and religious doctrine in a time alien to our own. Greenwich Village notes that its issues seem eerily contemporary, especially for women's rights. Galileo sets out to show how humans lived in a different universe than ours and thought about the nature of that universe and their place in it in vastly different terms than we do. Its rules are laid out to accomplish this objective. To prepare for a presentation and eventually trial statement, spontaneity is not the answer. Study is. The rules reinforce this message.

Stages of Power: Performance and Plotting

As in the last chapter concerning the number and assignment of roles, the rules in Stages aim for something in between those of Greenwich Village and Galileo. There is no trial at the center, but the queen's Privy Council opens each class with a formal ceremony, complete with Bible, bows, and curtseys. Most of each class is consumed with formal presentations to the council, which must decide whether to approve the performance of Marlowe's play, Shakespeare's work, or possibly neither. Rules for who may address the council—and therefore class—are strict and formal. Decorum and etiquette are essential. Skills in public presentation, and private petition writing, will go far.

But *Stages* encourages a lively backstage: students who represent actors have their own agendas in addition to seeing their company win the competition. It is not enough to get on stage after winning the council's approval; you have to have a starring role. Or perhaps your character is poor and willing to make somewhat gray arrangements with the other side if the price is right. Students on the Privy Council are free, indeed compelled, to engage in much behind-the-scenes maneuvering to ensure that, whatever the decision on which play, their long-standing opponents on the council lose influence by being on the wrong end of that decision. But under no circumstances will a member of the council allow any performance that the Queen and Crown might find objectionable in any way. *Stages* compels students to understand not just their roles, but the roles of other key players (and how to identify those players). Just as students in *Galileo* need to understand the context of their characters, those in *Stages* need to comprehend the sometimes labyrinthine maneuvers in Elizabeth's court—its rules.

To a great extent, the rules must reinforce the roles. How they do so can be different, and are especially so in *Great Power Rivalries*, in which each team of students, in effect, plays by a different set of rules.

Great Power Rivalries: Different Rules for Different Roles

Rivalries uses rules differently from most other classroom simulations. It is not a matter of size. Quite a few simulations include roles for nearly three dozen students. But few have eight different teams, and fewer have roles that compete against each other within the same team as well as worrying about what other teams have in store for them. I will use the same examples as in the previous chapter: Germany, France, the United States, and China.

Germany: Disagreements inside Dictatorship

Germany might seem to be the model of a juggernaut, all roles pulling toward the same goal: Nazi world domination with the subjugation and possible extermination of those races beneath the perfect Aryan. Actually, tension is built into the German team from the outset. Some of that tension is open and immediate, some subtle and long-term.

Finance Minister Schacht and SS leader Himmler will quickly find themselves at loggerheads. Himmler wants to press for a solution to the Jewish Question as rapidly as possible. That solution demands the devotion of considerable German resources to expand the SS, and even more resources to ensure German control over territories in Europe home to many Jews. Schacht considers war risky in the extreme and a financial calamity for certain. He also finds Nazi racial policy repugnant and thuggish. Army general von Manstein hardly objects to a bigger army in the name of war preparations, and will not shirk from war if Hitler orders it, but he is deeply uneasy over the creation and expansion of what he sees as a rival military organization to the army in Himmler's SS.

The roles dictate conflicting goals. But the rules guarantee actual conflict. Germany has only so much funding. It will go to the army or the SS or civilian objectives. Germany has only so many Bid Points in the simulation to attempt the implementation of various Policy Options. Preparing the SS to move toward a Final Solution and then implementing that solution requires hoards of these points. Using them is also a zero-sum affair.

The rules not only put German roles into conflict, they also give each role ways to pursue individual goals. Himmler can point to one rule that explicitly requires Germany to solve the Jewish Question or lose the simulation. Schacht is given the power to significantly increase Germany's budget, or to halt that increase if the government's choice of policies displeases him. Rules reinforce roles.

France: Discord in a Democracy

But rules do not always make roles simple. Each French role, whether Thorez, Blum, Daladier, Laval, Reynaud, or Bonnet, may share a common dread of a possible new war with Germany, but they each differ on how best to avoid such a war. Above all else, each leader is certain about how best to achieve that goal: become prime minister of France himself. The rules decree that France must hold elections every year, which translates into class time of at least once every week. It is impossible to overstate the significance of this one simple rule. Every French decision, from foreign policy to military spending, becomes subordinate to the scramble to do well in those elections. Thorez will adhere to his communist ideology. Blum will try to be a true socialist. The rest will wheel and deal with considerable flexibility and intrigue. But whether questions of ideology or intrigue prevail, every student character must learn how to run a successful political campaign. Running a campaign in a classroom simulation requires carefully thought-out rules for doing so.

Politics in democracies are complex. Elections are seldom less so. How can a classroom simulation adequately reproduce the environment of the French Third Republic in ways that are historically realistic yet manageable for students, and on a weekly basis to boot?

In fact, the election simulation-within-the-simulation must be more than simply realistic and feasible. It must be fair. It must operate in a way that does not rely on luck or instructor fiat, either of which not only kills the historical feel of things but also leads straight to student resentment and worse.

My solution has been to recognize that elections are contests to win the support of various constituencies, and that those contests, like elections overall, are zero-sum games. It does not matter how many candidates court the labor vote, for example, or how arduously. Great effort might increase labor's turnout, but no amount of effort will increase the number of labor voters overall. So, at each election, the various leaders in France adhere to these procedures:

Elections may result in one of four ways:

If a government cannot be formed immediately after a prior election
If the premier calls elections
If one year has passed since the last election
If a Policy Option outcome requires elections

Members of the National Assembly are controlled fully by their leaders. Their exact numbers will change in reaction to events in the simulation and the reactions of their leaders to those events. At the start of the simulation, the assembly breakdown is:

Laval: 100
Reynaud: 82

Daladier: 110
Blum: 149
Thorez: 72
Bonnet: 65
(TOTAL: 610)

Election Procedures

Of course, in assembly elections one runs only for a simple seat for oneself and, for the purposes of this simulation, victory is guaranteed.

What matters far more is how many assembly members are in your faction.

Once it has been determined that an election must be held, policy makers will have until the next class session to devise an election strategy and then commit Campaign Points to implement that strategy.

The number of Campaign Points available equals each policy maker's number of Clout Points times ten, but the policy maker with the highest number of Clout Points has these reduced by 20 percent and with the lowest raised by 20 percent. EXAMPLE: Blum goes into an election with 149 Clout Points, the highest. He would end up with 80 percent of 149 times ten, or 1192 Campaign Points for the election. Bonnet has 65 Clout Points, so ends up with 780 Campaign Points.[1]

Campaign Points are spent courting the support of voting blocs. These are[2]

Farmers
Sans-culottes
Artisans
Homemakers
Shopkeepers
Professionals
Intelligentsia
Business leaders
Patriots

Each bloc may be courted by simply spending Campaign Points on it. The more points spent, the likelier a higher percentage of that bloc will elect a member of your faction to the assembly. Likely, but not guaranteed— as you must compete with other policy makers. The more they spend, the more you must just to stay even. Should you compete hard for the big voting blocs that everyone else will be courting, or focus your efforts toward smaller blocs in which you are likely to see little, or less, competition? Hmm.

GENERAL ELECTION CAMPAIGNING GUIDE

It is impossible to overstate the importance of doing as well as you possibly can in any election. The size and strength of your political base is determined by each election and cannot be changed until the next election. And, the bigger your base, the more Campaign Points you have to expand it even further during the next election. Besides all that, your base determines how many Clout Points you have to affect your nation's policies in between elections.

No matter whether you start an election at the top of the pile or the bottom, there are a few basic tips you can try to maximize your chances:

> Try to invest Campaign Points among your natural political constituencies (see the Master Spreadsheet [British_Election, French_Election, or US congressional tab]). If you are British Labour, for example, be sure to invest in labour groups.
>
> Likewise, don't waste Campaign Points investing in groups that hate you. If you are a Southern segregationist in the US, African Americans aren't likely to vote for you no matter how many Campaign Points you devote to them.
>
> Always try to invest in other constituencies that you think your rivals are ignoring. If you are the *only* campaigner spending Campaign Points on shopkeepers, for instance, you will do very well with them.

These election procedures involve no luck. Very seldom will the instructor take a hand (usually necessary only early in the simulation if a student completely misunderstands the election procedure). Elections are easy for a student to understand and, as important, simple for the instructor to resolve swiftly and simply, utilizing that miracle of modern civilization, the spreadsheet.

My full simulation spreadsheet is available upon request. The relevant sheet or tab on it is French Election. Briefly, each constituency has a weight—how significant it is within the overall electorate. Each has an inclination. Workers will repay the attentions of a Thorez or a Blum well, but will be relatively unreceptive to anyone on the right. Patriots are the opposite. It will make sense for someone like Laval to invest Campaign Points to win them. Yet ignoring any constituency carries real risks, as that ignorance effectively concedes 100 percent of it to anyone investing even minimally.

These simulated election procedures allow for a wide range of outcomes for each faction, but a range based entirely on student decisions.

Once the voters have spoken, the same principle applies to forming a government. Each student will hold a precise number of members of parliament. Enough students have to agree to form a government (and who is to hold which office in that government) or fresh elections must be held without delay. This fact, in both reality and simulation, favors characters more in the center. But it is not impossible, or even unlikely, for a Popular Front coalition to be forged between Thorez and Blum, as occurred historically.

This election mechanism has worked smoothly both to replicate the political maneuverings that characterized France in the 1930s and to ensure that each student understands the implications of being a policy maker in a democracy. It also, quite deliberately, ensures that students with roles in a democracy have to pay much more attention to their domestic rivals, and in the far greater detail that periodic elections require, than those in dictatorships. The simulation's rules ensure that France, as a democracy, has problems Germany does not. Democratic roles need democratic rules. Democratic rules reinforce democratic roles. But democracies do not always abide by the same democratic rules. A very different sort of democratic problem arises in presidential polities such as the United States.

The United States: Democratic Hegemony?

The US team in *Rivalries* has Roosevelt literally presiding over a mix of four real characters representing something of a composite of US perspectives. Robert Taft is a traditional conservative at home and noninterventionist abroad. Richard Russell likes Roosevelt's domestic reforms and activist foreign policy so long as US race relations, especially in the South, remain untouched. Hiram Johnson strongly favors many of Roosevelt's domestic initiatives but vehemently opposes any involvement in European affairs. Wendell Willkie has become disillusioned with those initiatives but sympathizes with Roosevelt's foreign policy.

These are all interesting roles, and they can compete for influence and Clout Points in the biennial congressional elections in the United States, using a model of courting constituencies similar to France's. But even if the student-Roosevelt ineptly weakens his own faction in congressional races, the fact remains that Roosevelt is president, with quite considerable powers, at least until the 1940 presidential vote. And the model used for parliamentary and congressional elections will not do for US presidential contests. Another set of rules—another subsimulation, this one for the United States—will be necessary.

At this point, many prospective simulation instructors will throw up their hands. Yet another special procedure has to be invented? The investment of time in drafting the simulation already has been considerable, and coming up with a simulation within the simulation just for US presidential elections seems like a lot of time for little result in the grand scheme of things.

But it isn't. If the United States must have a team in the simulation, and it does, then the historical realities of the United States must be captured in some fashion. But this capture does not demand that you start from scratch. There are other simulations out there. Many have been published commercially. Use them as your foundation and modify them to suit your needs. *Great Power Rivalries* itself is based on Australian Design Group's *Days of Decision*. Perhaps there is a commercial or academic design for US presidential contests that will save a lot of legwork.

There is. *1960: The Making of a President*, currently published by GMT Games, is an excellent re-creation of the Kennedy-Nixon contest of that year. It could be used out of the box for 1936, 1940, and 1944, with easy adjustments for different electoral votes per state (and none for Alaska or Hawaii, not yet states). *1960* uses custom cards tailored to the actual campaign that year. A little more tinkering can direct students to re-written text on those cards more appropriate to circa 1940. A civil rights card, for example, could be translated into an anti-lynching card. Or you could go whole hog, as I did, and have a custom deck of cards printed for you with your own custom text.

No matter how far you want to tailor your sim-within-sim of US presidential elections, you will find that playing them will completely consume the attention of the entire US team—just as they should, and did, in real history. The addition of the special range of domestic Policy Options, plus the periodic congressional and presidential elections, will keep students occupied, and eager to do more research on their characters throughout the semester, even if the United States never goes to war. Best of all, there is no dice rolling (although which presidential election cards are drawn, and when, introduces a random element). US presidential elections in *Rivalries* do give an edge to Roosevelt, but the students see them as both historically accurate and fair. These two ends, accuracy and fairness, appear to be at odds, though, in the final case of China.

China: Writing Rules for Severe Asymmetry

The Chinese "team"—actually three rivals, Jiang Jieshi, Mao Zedong, and Wang Jingwei, all at each other's throats—presents a great challenge for achieving both historical accuracy and fairness in the eyes of the students.

All three characters have the same two objectives: to make themselves ruler of China and to make China great again. But, at least for the former, Jiang holds staggering advantages as the simulation starts in 1936. He does not control all of China. Western and far southern provinces are ruled by local warlords, willing to ally with any leader if the price is right. Manchuria is under Japanese occupation, its former warlord eager for its return or at least revenge on Tokyo. Mao occupies a single province. Wang has none. Jiang's army is large, if not well trained. Mao's is tiny and ragged. Wang has no military at all. Not a guaranteed victory to seize control of China, perhaps, but a commanding position.

Rivalries' standard rules governing army warfare put Mao and Wang in impossible positions. Rules governing elections won't work, either. China does not have them. The roles are clear and important. Special rules will have to provide a way for Mao and Wang to have a chance to control their country, and do so in a historically plausible way and one that seems fair to the three students.

For Mao, history itself provides suggestions. Mao was able to survive 1936, and go on to victory twelve years later, because Jiang was forced to confront Japan—forced by regional warlords and leaders to do so and, by the summer of 1937, forced by the Japanese themselves after fighting broke out near the Marco Polo Bridge outside Beijing.

Good simulation designs avoid scripted reenactments. Simply ordering Jiang to back off Mao, or telling the Japanese team that they have to attack Jiang in 1937, will not do. Good simulation designs will drive the student to discover why Jiang acted as he did and, in this case, why he did not act to finish off Mao in 1936. Most student-Jiangs, in fact, find outright alliance with Japan highly attractive. Join forces, slay the communists

(Chinese and Russian), cement control of China, except for those northeastern portions reserved for the Japanese, live happily ever after. In many of my earlier runs of *Rivalries*, this is exactly what happened.

Should it have? Should the real Jiang have chosen condominium, albeit as a somewhat junior partner, with Japan? History argues otherwise. It was precisely because Jiang refused to confront Japan that led to the warlords' revolt, and popular Chinese pressure, against him culminating in the Xi'an Incident of 1936. So, I concluded, *Rivalries* needed a way to simulate the influence of popular and warlord influence on Jiang to be a nationalist in fact as well as name. Rather than dictate such pressure, I wrote a Policy Option for both Mao and Wang that, if they wish to attempt it, will prevent Jiang from initiating any formal understanding with Japan (through one of his own Policy Options) until dealing with public discontent (through a Policy Option that will require significant resources from Jiang). In addition, if Jiang proceeds thereafter to an understanding with the Japanese, Wang's position, and a possible bid for power, within the Chinese Nationalist Party is greatly strengthened. Jiang remains free to pursue his cooperation with Tokyo, but there will be costs and risks.

The rules of a simulation can be used to complicate roles, to force students to consider ramifications of their actions and move toward a deeper understanding of the characters they represent. Adding friction to a Jiang-Japan combination is one way to level the playing field within China. But so far those rules have done little to ensure Mao's survival at Jiang's hands even if Jiang lacks Japanese support. Nor do the Chinese communists, so far, have a realistic chance to win China, as they historically did.

Historically, though, the communists had no realistic chance in 1936. That chance arose after Jiang became embroiled in a war with Japan, that war proved prolonged, and the communists proved adept at organizing popular resistance, sometimes through guerrilla warfare, behind Japanese lines. Their aptitude in these regards, however, does not require a Jiang-Japan war in the simulation. Why not allow Mao to engage in resistance/guerrilla warfare directly against Jiang? All we need are rules to allow for such warfare—rules that will enhance Mao's role and encourage the student-Mao to look more deeply at the real character.

Scholarly literature on partisan warfare remains minuscule compared to conventional conflict, but it makes a compelling case for considering the role of irregular forces in the Second World War. To be sure, partisans existed before that war. The term *guerrilla* itself comes from the Spanish resistance against Napoleon's occupation force in the early nineteenth century. But partisan warfare was nearly as global as the conventional war of 1939 to 1945, with widespread resistance in the Soviet Union, Poland, Greece and Yugoslavia, France, and, most centrally, China. What is more remarkable, and rarely acknowledged in conventional studies, these resistance forces survived the most brutal methods that Nazi Germany (or Imperial Japan) could devise to obliterate them. Any simulation worth its salt ought to have a way to consider their role.

The first step in such a consideration is to ensure historical plausibility. Partisan forces during the Second World War rarely expelled conventional, occupying forces. Partisans did not achieve final victory on their own. That came from conventional forces either introduced from outside, as with France, or the return of in-country regular forces, as in the Soviet Union, or the conversion of guerrillas into conventional forces, as in Mao's China. The role of the partisan was to harass, to weaken through raiding, or to simply persist, to keep one's side in the fight and tie down the enemy occupier.

With this role in mind, I devised these rules for guerrilla warfare in China:

Only Mao (CCP) may ever buy or deploy partisans. He may do so once he or a Coalition China is at war with another Major Power or he is at war with another Chinese faction (Wang or Jiang).

Mao obtains for free, each turn, a number of partisan points equal to his current Political Effectiveness. In addition, Mao may purchase partisans from his current income of Clout Points, at a rate of 1 partisan point for 70 Clout Points.

These partisans may be deployed in any Chinese (or Manchurian) province occupied by the Major Power or Chinese faction that Mao is at war with, but never more per province than Mao's current Political Effectiveness.

Partisans may never be deployed in an enemy's Sanctuary province, whether the Sanctuary option has been set on or off.

If China establishes a Coalition China while Mao has partisans deployed, all partisan points in provinces Mao is not at war with are immediately converted to regular (Coalition) Army Points at standard conversion rates.

These procedures ensure a steady but limited supply of partisans that go "on map" and "raid," but never actually seize control of any provinces. Chinese partisans may be converted to regular forces that then use standard rules for army combat and can control territory. But this conversion is a one-way, irrevocable affair and one that bars the future use of partisan forces. Student-Mao will convert with great care and calculation, and hopefully deep study of history's Mao to see why it worked for him.[3]

With these additions to the rules of the simulation, Mao has a fighting chance even if he loses all his territory to Jiang early on. In fact, an early loss to Jiang, especially if Jiang does ally with the Japanese, offers Mao an especially wide arena for marshalling resistance forces. Rules can be used, sometimes must be used, to enhance the viability of roles.

Mao now has a chance, but what about Wang, who starts the simulation in an even weaker position and who does not have guerrilla skills at his disposal? How can we craft simulation rules that offer Wang possibilities without warping history?

Whereas Mao Zedong and Jiang Jieshi are well-known figures, both subjects of voluminous scholarship even in English, Wang Jingwei is unheard of and has little written about him. He was a leading figure in the Nationalist Party until the late 1920s, when Jiang eclipsed him. He remained at odds with Jiang thereafter, eventually agreeing to head a rival Chinese government in collaboration with the Japanese and based in Japanese-occupied China. Historically, this initiative went nowhere. Japan offered Wang little besides lip service. He died in 1944, receiving treatment in Japan for a failed assassination attempt against him. He was reviled as a traitor by both nationalists and communists.

When the hapless students who, in ignorance, draw Wang as their character in the simulation, they invariably fall into a mix of anger and resignation. What did they do to be consigned to a position of no power, no territory, and apparently no future for the entire semester? What are they supposed to do during class?

For most students representing Wang, the first impulse is to take a cue from history and rush to the Japanese team proposing that they war against Jiang and put Wang in power. Better a puppet than a pauper. This approach rarely succeeds, as Wang has nothing to offer the Japanese besides a pauper as a puppet. So far, my rules allow Wang to be able to hamstring an alliance between Jiang and Japan, but this is scant consolation for any student playing Wang. Like Mao, Wang needs a chance to rule China. It is up to the simulation's rules for China to provide him one.

China's history again suggests a way: those regional warlords. It would be ham-handed and ahistorical simply to assign them to Wang. But, as the Xi'an Incident of 1936 demonstrated, the warlords were hardly in Jiang's pocket. What if they could be courted by Wang, or for that matter Mao and Jiang? The result would be one more worry for Jiang. Mao could go for the warlords, but doing so would divert his resources from fostering a resistance. Wang would have something to pursue with the prospect of victory, or at least territory, or at least leverage. Interesting possibilities open up.

Introducing regional warlords is historical, but it opens a host of complications. How many should there be? Since they will not have students to represent them, how should their armies and resources be treated? How easy should their courtship be, and should it be equally easy for Wang, Mao, and Jiang? You can consult *Rivalries'* master files to see how I answered these questions in detail.[4] Here, I want to stress the central point of this chapter.

Designing a simulation, whether it is for one class or the entire semester, requires the designer to assume the perspective of each and every student position, to ask if the objectives and means available to that character reflect his or her historical counterpart's accurately, or at least plausibly, and gives every student options, hope, and things to worry about. A key component of any simulation's design is its rules.

4

REQUIREMENTS

Students enjoy simulations. They come to class. They participate actively. They stay late. They talk to each other after each class to eagerly prepare for the next one. But what do they learn?

As all instructors realize, this question has two parts. We first need to know what we want to teach. Then we want to figure out how to judge how successfully we have taught it to each student.

How we teach can be *what* we teach. We all strive to engage our students, to involve them actively in class. That is why we might pause during lecture and invite questions, why we have small recitation sections in our big lecture courses, why we might gather students into small groups in those recitations to consider problems or assignments jointly. We do these things because interaction itself is learning. It may be fine if students sit, start of class to finish, simply taking notes. But it is much better if they think about their subjects, and even better if they think about those subjects with others.

And still better if they think about those subjects from the perspective of someone else. A simulation, by its very nature, is a learning experience:

> The structure of the course puts an emphasis on knowing the other players from the moment everything begins—you want to know yourself the best of course, but staying up late researching obscure bits of writing by an opponent which may be used to convince them that they might be more partial to your cause was equally important. Primary sources became the currency of deal making. "I know a way you could convince so-and-so to give you that thing you need" was everywhere, but bad information was hand-waived in favor of someone who could make a better case with higher quality documentation. The genius of the course structure is that by giving the students a game, we all became historians—coming up with theories of what historical figures might have believed in, and fighting to qualify and prove that position to others using the best sources we could find. In the process of trying to win the Simulation, I learned in a highly personal way the goals, beliefs, passions, and limitations of a large cadre of important figures and governments, which I remember precisely even more than ten years later. I have never taken another course that was so successful at teaching so much in such a short time frame.[1]

Students in a simulation can interact more freely with each other, moreover, precisely because they are their characters, not themselves. There is no need to divulge personal details of any kind. There are no breaches of personal privacy.

To be sure, students in *Greenwich Village* will learn about how women and workers were treated a century ago. *Galileo* should open minds about how profoundly disturbing his theories were to how fellow humans conceived of their place in the order of things. *Stages* will allow students to see behind the curtain of Elizabethan society and politics. *Rivalries* introduces them to political and military conflict in ways more vivid than any (one hopes) will experience in real life.

But, in a wider way, simply having students talk, reason, and argue with each other is itself an inimitable learning experience for them, regardless of the simulation's formal subject matter.

Even so, the fact remains that, whether as briefer exercises as part of a regular class or as a semester-long class itself, a simulation—like any other course component—needs requirements, manifestations of a student's learning that the instructor can evaluate. Like it or not, grades are a part of academia. And grades are the formal manifestation of the instructor's evaluation.

Evaluation is not unique to simulations, of course. But evaluation in a simulation is quite different than in a more conventional course. There is no common basis, from lectures or readings, for a common examination. There is no single yardstick for evaluation in a simulation. How are Galileo and the church to be judged, or Marlowe or Shakespeare, or the workers and suffragists of *Greenwich Village*? How can *Rivalries'* Roosevelt, Schacht, Blum, or Mao (or poor Wang) be graded on anything like similar measurements?

This lack of commonality disturbs some students. And nearly all students are anxious about their standing in—their grade for—their classes. In a simulation, there is no set, sit-down examination or other common assignment for evaluation. There is something better: students quickly pick up how well their characters, or teams, are doing on a day-to-day, sometimes minute-by-minute, basis. In *Stages*, Marlowe's proposed lead just gave an impassioned presentation that showed off his acting chops? Shakespeare's troupe knows right away that they will have to come up with something to top it. In *Rivalries*, Himmler just persuaded Hitler to invest major resources in the SS? Schacht will have to consider whether to change Hitler's mind or adjust to new realities and resign as Finance Minister, with further thought how to explain this setback in his journal.

While grades have their place, the beauty of simulations is to make clear to students how well they are doing without staring at the A-to-F on their latest assignment or exam. If not well, they often will want to talk to you to figure out how to do better. This is a far better way for them to learn, and you to teach, than that single red letter.[2]

Your evaluations, during and after the simulation, have to be on an individual basis. But this does not mean that student assignments—class requirements—have to be. A common element to nearly all classroom simulations is public address of some kind. *Greenwich Village* structures presentations rather formally. One class session is devoted to speeches by suffragists, followed by questions or comments from students in other groups, such as labor. Another gives labor organizers their say with questions from suffragists. A third features a Feminist Mass Meeting, and so on. *Galileo* offers several sessions for arguments for and against its central character. *Stages* has formal debates before the queen's Privy Council to advocate for Marlowe or Shakespeare.

Great Power Rivalries has no formal speaking requirement. Every student will advocate in every class session, but usually only in front of their national teammates. Foreign ministers will be tasked with making presentations to potential allies or enemies. On occasion, a head of state will call for an international summit, a Munich or a Yalta of some kind, and there formal presentations wholly organized by the students will take place. *Rivalries* has also seen its share of war crimes trials, again organized by students and invariably riveting (just ask Laval or von Manstein). There is plenty of argument and speechmaking, but not often before the class as a whole and the arguments and speeches are much more driven in timing and substance by the students themselves. Great stuff for student interaction, but impossible for the instructor to observe in its entirety.

Students speak to persuade their peers to cooperate with their objectives in class. Students write to persuade instructors that they have learned something from class. *Greenwich Village* links speaking and writing closely. Most of its writing assignments prepare for presentations, although at least one is meant for simulated publication in Max Eastman's *The Masses* magazine. *Galileo* stresses mastery of material in a similar fashion. *Stages* does likewise but, as with *Greenwich Village*, requires at least one "strategic imaginative writing" for circulation to all other players, with the intriguing option that it can be anonymous.[3]

Rivalries has a more formal, and longer, set of writing assignments, as might be expected from a simulation running the length of the semester. It departs from most simulations in requiring students to research and write their own role sheets, which are due very early in the course to ensure that the students understand their characters. Students also must record in-character journals for the duration of the simulation. Students write these in first person, often in colorful ways. One student-Stalin wrote a letter to his mistress after each class, the collection forming his journal. A student-Wang "sent" postcards to her character's friends back in China, a clever device since her character turned out to spend most of the semester in exile. A von Manstein, from a Germany that collapsed at about the same time the real Third Reich had, carefully stained his journal's pages brown with tea leaves, then burned holes in them, binding the sum in hemp twine with a cover note from a Soviet soldier explaining its circumstances of discovery from the ruins of the Third Reich.

These journals are central to my evaluation of student performance: what they have learned from the simulation, and what grade they will get for the course. Unlike live interactions, where the instructor can only observe one place (or one team) at a time, student writings (like actual historical documents) can be absorbed at pace, and an understanding of what happened (here, in the simulation) can be gleaned.

Even so, grading performances, speaking or written, in a simulation is far different than in most college courses. The root of this difference is the very asymmetrical positions that students find themselves in. Grading students in simulations requires new thinking about how to evaluate student learning. Instructors have employed different grading methods for decades. Comparing these methods can offer insights into grading students in a simulation. To use just one example:

A Tale of Two Teachers

Professor Zlotnick[4] was a rising star in my major's Department of Public Address and Group Communication. As might be expected, he gave captivating lectures, invariably well prepared, timed to the minute, beginning and ending with a clear outline of their important themes. In an age before PowerPoint, they were a notetaker's dream.

Professor Leonard was a seasoned, renowned historian. By the time I arrived on campus, he did not lecture any longer. He offered just large discussion-only courses of about forty students. Because his classroom had a traditional seat layout, he had student volunteers, on a rotating basis, come to class twenty minutes early to rearrange chairs and tables. He posted discussion questions on a blackboard (a real blackboard, not the electronic kind), but otherwise his classes were unstructured and highly dependent on student preparation and participation. He gave a midterm and final examination, just as Professor Zlotnick did, but preparing for them was more difficult because of the less structured nature of Leonard's discussions compared to the well-organized lectures of Zlotnick.

Professor Zlotnick was a stickler for fairness toward his students. He also coached the university's debate team and had a number of its members in his classes. So as to avoid possible favoritism, he barred students from writing their names on their exams. Instead, each student took a number as she or he entered the exam room, wrote that number on the booklet, and submitted name and number to a teaching assistant, who kept both confidential until after Professor Zlotnick completed grading the exams.

For reasons that became clear to me only years later, Professor Leonard made it a point to know exactly whose name was on each exam. Not for simple identification, but to know by what standards he should judge the examination itself. Was the student a senior, majoring in history, who had taken several of his courses before? Or was it a sophomore's first, and maybe last, history course? Professor Leonard knew. He took care to look over each student's academic records and—his trump card—he had those twenty minutes of set-up time with each student, one-on-one, before his classes, to find out a bit about the student's background and hopes.

Two examinations of exactly the same quality could receive entirely different grades from Professor Leonard. He would have higher standards for the history senior but be more forgiving, and more encouraging, for the novice sophomore. His comments on exam essays reflected those standards.

Which method better evaluates student progress? Which is more fair? A simulation forces the instructor to confront these questions directly. Should a student-Wang be held to the same standards as a student-Hitler? Should the instructor take these asymmetries into account not just in grading students at the end of the course, but assigning student roles at the beginning? If so, should the equivalent of the history seniors be given (or get stuck with) Wangs or Hitlers?

Whatever the answers each instructor gives to these questions, it is useful to ask them, because so few instructors do ask them of their students in their traditional courses. It might be enough to recognize a student's face while crossing paths on campus for most teachers. But, if you teach a course with a simulation, faces are not enough. In a simulation, students act within teams, but your evaluation of them must be an entirely individualized affair. Your grading has to be asymmetric.

This very asymmetry bothers many of my students. It is easy to understand why. Most college courses teach symmetrically. Students start the first day of class on an even footing, are exposed to the same lecture or recitation experiences, and take the same examinations. Some instructors will even make available sample or model examinations of varying quality so that students can see what the instructor grades highly.

Not so a simulation. Students begin in wildly disparate positions depending on which character they represent. Hitler has a team, an army, and a robust budget from the beginning. Wang has fierce rivals, not one soldier, and an income of zero. Like it or not, *Stages'* student-Shakespeare has an edge over rival Marlowe, because whoever heard of Marlowe? At least for most students, Galileo is a farsighted scientist, the Catholic Church of his time an assortment of stiff-necked bigots.

This disparity is not just a matter of resources, either. Student-Zhukov can become the cleverest army commander in any simulation ever taught, but if student-Stalin is a clown, the Soviet Union will not do well. Student-Taft can fight a brilliant delaying action to keep the United States out of war, but if Roosevelt is cunning, or if Japan attacks Hawaii, Taft's core goal in the simulation will not be achieved no matter how well his student represented and played her character's position.

Students, especially those representing Wang, Zhukov, or Taft in the examples above, will openly worry that they will fail the course through no fault of their own. No other single subject consumes more of my office hours during a semester when I teach *Great Power Rivalries*, as one student after another comes in to privately ask what more they can do with their own characters or how they can override the bad judgment or moves of their characters' foolish teammates.

I address these worries with three answers. Has the student accurately captured her or his character's perspective, motives, and goals in their biographical papers (role sheets) they wrote early in the semester? Do they recall a similar sense of helplessness in Wang, after he lost control of the Chinese nationalists, or Zhukov, the day after Germany's crushing initial invasion victories, or Taft, when he learned of Pearl Harbor? Did any of their historical characters give up and refuse to carry on? How did they adjust to their setbacks or failures?

I also stress that, at least in the case of the simulation, they really can get that proverbial A for effort. But they have to demonstrate that effort.

Since I cannot keep a close eye at all times on all thirty-five students across four rooms, I need to see evidence of that effort in the journals the students give me at the end of the simulation. Like real-history memoirs, these journals should attempt to portray their authors in best light and, hence, in as much detail as possible. I read (and grade) them as memoirs, in fact, comparing what each member of a team said about a given event or development within that team during the semester. Since the students write their journals in the first person, the results are often extraordinarily detailed, such as Stalin's long letters to his mistress after every class or Wang's postcards from exile. A Mussolini memoir included an astounding amount of historical detail, revealing the depth of research on that character that the student had done throughout the semester but with special and sometimes hilarious vignettes about specific episodes that occurred during the semester. Of course, there is a downside to this method of evaluation as well. One Mao was spectacularly successful in becoming China's ruler with an amazing mix of diplomacy, negotiation, guerrilla tactics, and finally conventional conquest. Just like the real Mao! But the student was so engaged in these activities that he neglected his journal, which was thin and often skipped over years at a time. As history's Churchill well knew, it is not enough to simply do very well. One must persuade the world that one has done very well. If you want to get a good grade in *Rivalries*, you need to write a journal demonstrating your effort and justifying your decisions. If you want to make history, become a historian.

The third answer I give to my worried students also blurs the line between simulation and reality. Most have jobs in addition to their studies. I ask if they ever had a coworker who goofed off or was simply incompetent. Or a supervisor who was clueless, petty, or just plain cruel. Pretty much everyone had. How had they handled their situation at work? Pretty much everyone had soldiered on. Some picked up the slack of bad colleagues. Some took on supervisor responsibilities, giving more time without more pay. Or they had gone about their business even with an unpleasant boss. By the time our conversation was over, they understood my point about their woes on their simulation team. The line between class simulation and contemporary, real-world reality is often fuzzier than first appears.

In fact, after hearing quite a few of students' stories about problems at work, I began to consider how poorly most college courses prepare them for real life. Training and knowledge are superbly useful, to be sure. Skills, from writing to the laboratory, can be taught and improved. But two fundamental premises of nearly all courses are that all students start on an equal basis and must be evaluated using identical criteria. A score of 95 on an exam is an A; a 35 is an F—no matter whose name is on the booklet cover.

For pure knowledge and training courses, this is a necessary state of affairs. You either know organic chemistry or you don't. You either know where the pituitary gland is or you don't. You either have the details in your head, and know how to read them on a screen or in your patient's body, to conduct surgery safely or you have no place in the operating room.

But in preparation for other walks of life, a rigid, fixed yardstick of evaluation in a college course seems a poor way to judge student suitability or progress. Simulations demand the Professor Leonard treatment, and even extend it. It becomes essential for the instructor to come to know each student closely, from classroom observation to a careful reading of that student's journal. As their journals will reveal, students too have to come to know each other closely—or rather to know each other's characters closely—and to work together despite different outlooks and goals. Student engagement is not just with the instructor or class material. A vital part of that engagement occurs among the students themselves. The instructor's evaluation of the student will depend not just on mastery of material but also each student's ability to attempt to use that mastery to interact successfully with other students. The instructor's grading becomes highly individualized, and rightly so. No student left alike.

5

ROOM

In one important way, high school teachers have a big advantage over their "higher ed" counterparts. Most college instructors are itinerants. Whether we are tenured faculty or part-time adjuncts dashing from campus to campus, we do not teach in the same room every day, every semester, to rotating sets of students. We do not have a desk in the classroom to store our teaching aids in, nor a wall to hang posters or maps from. We take whatever space we are assigned for class and commute there from our offices, if we have one of those. We do not think much about the spaces in which we teach, unless they have particularly bad acoustics, poor layouts, bad heating or cooling, or spectacular window views likely to distract our students.

The room factor works against the objectives of any simulation. The space in which a simulation takes place is not as important as its roles or rules, perhaps, but it matters. What if *Greenwich Village* could be held in the real Greenwich Village, or at least around a café or coffee house that looks like it did in 1913? What if you could hold *Galileo* in a courtroom, better yet, one with seventeenth-century ecclesiastical trappings? Or have a similar venue, with raised benches and the Elizabethan works for the queen's Privy Council in *Stages*?

Decorating the classroom can be a real challenge. Dragging the necessary accoutrements, be they Bibles, royal stamps and seals, properly emblazoned podiums, or period-accurate coffee tables, is beyond the physical abilities of most of us. Then there is the issue of where to store these items between uses. Neither broom closet nor car trunk seem very attractive alternatives.

Decorating the students is rather easier. *Greenwich Village* takes pains to impart the flavor of place and time by directly rewarding student costume and decoration. Any instructor offering a simulation should imitate this effort as far as possible. *Greenwich Village* has a bit of an edge since suffragist colors are readily available (even if bloomers are not), and a reasonable facsimile of working-class coveralls and such can be readily had, often in students' existing wardrobes. Posters and handmade signs can be easily crafted, and their storage is not the instructor's problem.

Galileo and *Stages* are not quite so straightforward. But costuming their students is not impossible, either, with a little imagination. Academic gowns remain a bit pricey on e-Bay, especially the doctorate versions. But high school gowns are in plentiful supply. Better yet, some students might still have theirs. Dark-colored bedsheets might do in a pinch. True miters, for bishops on up, are rather expensive, but budget models are available, or a little needlework with scratch materials might do the trick.

Why bother at all with these fluffs? Because clothing might not make the man, but it absolutely does create an impression or environment. Try this for yourself: teach one class in jeans, a T-shirt, and flip-flops, another in sport coat, tie, and dress shoes or equivalent. Notice any difference in student reactions and demeanor?

The effect is even more pronounced when students dress themselves for class. Simulations can be designed to encourage costume. *Greenwich Village* explicitly does so through Personal Influence Point awards. *Galileo* is a bit subtler, though it does devote a class session to a party hosted by Prince Cesi at his palace in Rome. No flip-flops there. *Stages* might not have parties, but it can have performances, perhaps in accurate dress.

Often, students will provide props and costumes spontaneously. *Rivalries* has seen Japan's part of the fascist room festooned with the Rising Sun flag and *hachimaki*. Students on past Soviet teams have scribbled communist slogans on their room's chalkboard. One brought in a bust of Stalin for every class. Student-Maos took to wearing the distinctive cadet-style cap with red star. On several occasions, Franklin Roosevelt entered the democracies' room in a wheelchair. French and British team members took to wearing trench coats, and Chamberlain carried his trademark umbrella. Somewhat disturbingly, I have had a Hitler grow that mustache. Another Hitler dressed in a Wehrmacht (though not SS) uniform for the final class retrospective, prompting a real test of campus tolerance and at least one phone call to the university constabulary.

Costume Caveats

Some of these examples illustrate a kind of equivalency between emotional and disturbing language, as discussed in "Nazis in the Classroom" (chapter 2) and troubling costumery. Some—like anything close to Nazism—are obvious. Even a regular German army uniform elicited gapes even from students in the simulation class, let alone from the stroll around campus.

Others can be obvious in retrospect. Roosevelt's wheelchair debut elicited cries of amusement as things turned out. But what if a student who uses a wheelchair had been in the simulation? Or simply in the hallway when student-FDR was wheeled about? The other students on the US team, who had cooked up the scheme (and borrowed the wheelchair), had not thought of that possibility. I didn't scold them for that, but I did ask them why the actual Roosevelt had gone to considerable (and literal) pains not to be seen in his chair.

Even those trench coats and umbrellas can pose difficulties. In my *Rivalries*, every historical character, with the exception perhaps of Mao Zedong's Zhongshan suit, was dressed in western-style clothing or uniforms. But there are some simulations in which costumes could emphasize strong cultural identities, identities that can rub raw in the modern classroom. No one would ask students representing slaves to dress the part. But what about Reacting simulations such as *Forest Diplomacy: Cultures in Conflict on the Pennsylvania Frontier, 1757* or *Red Clay, 1835: Cherokee*

Removal and the Meaning of Sovereignty? Should the students in Delaware or Cherokee roles dress accordingly? What would Native American students make of their doing so? What about the student in the role of Gandhi in *Defining a Nation: India on the Eve of Independence, 1945*: shawl, dhoti, and sandals?[1]

Costumes can enhance the simulation experience. But unlike roles—which require students' immersion in them—costumes are optional. They should not be required of any student. Each instructor and simulation designer needs to give forethought to whether some should be banned outright, or whether their use should be turned into a teachable moment, as with FDR's wheelchair.

Immersion Space

It is not just costumes that can create a sense of immersion in a simulation. Many other possibilities exist to enhance the simulation experience. Years ago I began putting photographs of each role on the various national team course packs in *Great Power Rivalries*. At first I thought it fairly trivial, but soon learned that the photos spurred the students to discover the person behind the picture. Bringing props to class also moves students to learn more about the country and culture of their characters. My most successful by far has been my (unsharpened) Japanese replica of a *tantō* dagger used for ritual suicide.

In *Rivalries*, the environment plays a crucial role in other regards as well. As noted in the introduction, it uses four separate rooms with strict rules for who can travel among them. Creative use of space can be combined with simulation rules and roles to enhance the immersive effect. Communication is easy among teams of the same ideology—Germany, Italy, and Japan sit in the fascists' room; Britain, France, and the US in the democracies' room—but across ideologies, including the isolated Soviet team, is more sporadic and difficult. Heads of state[2] cannot leave their home rooms.[3] They have foreign ministers to do that for them, further complicating communication across ideologies.[4] The distinction might appear trivial, an impression belied by the seriousness of the students traversing the hallways, and the suspicion among their heads of state that somehow the right message is not getting through.

Space—here, separate rooms to isolate students on different national teams—can be used in still other ways to enhance student roles. The Soviet team sits alone, reflecting the strong anti-communist environment globally in the 1930s. But two non-Soviet characters are granted full access to visit Moscow any time they wish: China's Mao Zedong and France's Maurice Thorez, both communists themselves. This simple mechanic dramatically raises anti-Red suspicions among the democracies in particular. Thorez can sit either among them or with the Soviets, and can come and go as he pleases. Is he passing information or leaking plans? These suspicions make for interesting choices for student-Thorez. Should she or he use suspicion as a stick over the heads of other members of the French team, blustering and threatening unless French policy adjusts? Or should student-Thorez soft-pedal that suspicion, insisting on their loyalty to France? This choice, apparent to all students ever taking the role of Thorez, prompts additional research into the choices the historical character actually made, as comfortless as some of them were.

Student-Maos face similar decisions. They can use the threat, or bluff, of imminent Soviet aid as a club over their Chinese rivals to buy concessions or at least time. But a too-aggressive use of this tool can trigger Jiang or Wang to play the anti-communist card and obtain aid of their own from either the fascists or the democracies, or conceivably both.

Creative use of space can enhance roles, and so the simulation itself. *Greenwich Village*, for example, might provide separate rooms for unionists and suffragists for private organizing, strategizing, and practicing presentations at Polly's, and ideally a separate space for Polly's itself. *Galileo* could arrange something similar for its various scholarly and clerical factions. *Stages* would offer three venues. Two for the two actors' companies, and one for the queen's Privy Council, which could be reserved for private maneuvering among its members when it was not in formal session to hear arguments from the companies. Thinking about space as an instructional tool opens many possibilities, and not just for instructors.

How Big a Room? The Upper Limits on a Simulation's Size

As with effective classroom discussions, there tends to be an upper limit on the number of students able to participate in an effective simulation.

Most simulations being run today[5] suggest ten to thirty roles. Some can accommodate up to fifty. A very few run higher. It is not hard to see why. As with discussions, it is important to try to involve every student actively. Doing so in a class of ninety or two hundred ranges from challenging to impossible.

But the very nature of a simulation does suggest possibilities. Because students tend to "run themselves" with relatively little direct involvement from the instructor, a very large simulation could work with teams that are themselves sized to encourage small-group participation. Nicolas Proctor has designed a simulation of the Democratic National Convention in Chicago, 1968, that can readily accept over fifty students because they can be broken into small groups of protestors (themselves factionalized into subteams), party delegates, and journalists.[6] Press conferences and news stories (and the quest to have your group or boss favorably featured in them) dominate much of the proceedings, culminating in the writing of the party's platform. *Chicago, 1968* as a simulation can be something of a nine-ring circus, requiring fairly nimble coordination and scheduling of wider events on the part of the instructor. Then again, the actual Chicago convention was something of a circus, too.

Student-Made Spaces

A sure sign of a successful course is students eager to work on it and talk about it outside of actual class sessions. That sometimes happens with conventional courses. It always happens with simulations. It happened with nighttime phone calls in the 1980s, midnight emails by the late nineties, video conferencing a decade later, then social media and beyond. But it also happens with face-to-face meetings on campus or even off, with students hosting team get-togethers that frequently feature team-related decorations and food.[7] In *Rivalries*, student journals often give the instructor a fascinating look at what students do about their course material outside of class.

Sometimes instructors find these student meetings disturbing. What if *Greenwich Village*'s leading suffragist and top union organizer are best friends in their lives as students? *Galileo*'s lead character and the pope could be real-life roommates. *Stages*' key characters might be on the same sports team or other student organization. It may be fine that Thorez has split loyalties in *Rivalries*, but not so good if student-Himmler and student-Stalin are best buddies in real life. The possibilities for mischief and betrayal seem significant. Either will spoil the immersive goal of the simulation. Corralling these potential problems is one of the duties of the "almighty instructor."

6

The A.I.

No, not Artificial Intelligence. It might seem odd to use the phrase "Almighty Instructor" since an ideal simulation would have its instructor act only as a largely passive observer. Perfect construction of roles and rules would render intervention or supervision unnecessary. Listening to student presentations and reading their papers would remain instructor responsibilities. But for all intents and purposes, the students would run the simulation themselves.

My colleagues at Stony Brook are perennially amazed that such actually occurs in *Great Power Rivalries*. They pass the democracy or fascist rooms and see students busily conducting discussions or debates with no instructor present. They notice foreign ministers involved in intense hallway negotiations with me nowhere to be seen.

For the most part, most simulations do run themselves. But there are a number of possibilities, some unlikely, others not, that any instructor has to prepare for and respond to. Sometimes intervention is necessary.

Enforcer of Rules, Reminder of Roles

First, the instructor must enforce the simulation's rules. For example, many simulations focus on presentations and advocacy. Some students will take naturally to these activities. Some will try to monopolize them. Still others will attempt to avoid them. The instructor needs to interpret the rules of the simulation accordingly. If the simulation requires a speech from every student, podium time has to be reserved and enforced. If it does not, other assignments for students shy of the spotlight need to be arranged. Many of these kinds of simulations have a "podium rule": if a student who has not said anything to the class approaches the podium, she or he must be given a swift opportunity to speak. The instructor has to enforce this rule.

Other simulations, including my *Rivalries*, receive student input through the submission of a set of each nation's political, economic, and military decisions on a formal turnsheet due at the end of each class. These decisions will be at the center of intense student debate during class. Often, students will reach no compromise on these decisions as the end of class approaches. Without turnsheets from all teams, a turn cannot be run. The instructor must enforce deadlines rigorously and permit no amendments after them—unless she or he is amenable to midnight emails or similar shenanigans.

A second key duty of the instructor is reinforcing student roles. Part of this duty is police work. If a simulation requires structure or protocols, the instructor has to see these obeyed. *Stages of Power* stipulates that each Privy Council session begin with all men with heads bowed, women performing the curtsy, as the councillors enter. Then Councillor Whitgift leads the room in prayer, Bible in hand. All present must show respect for the councillors, their betters—no "all men created equal" business here. A *Greenwich Village* villager referring to or using a cellphone needs a reminder. A conservative cardinal in *Galileo* who decides that heresy is laudable if it promotes new ways of thinking needs a holy visitation. A Himmler in *Rivalries* expressing tolerance for the lesser races requires one from the nether realm.

In and Out—of Character

As these last examples indicate, most of an instructor's interventions involve keeping students in their roles. Careful thought on how the simulation initially assigns these roles can avoid many headaches later on. But not all. Two problems recur with some regularity.

In long simulations like *Rivalries*, or shorter ones like *Galileo* that compress time, students may become confused about their roles because they are forced to jump into a new character's skin. *Galileo* leaps from 1616 to 1632 in midsimulation, and acknowledges the passage of time with a Grim Reaper Lottery[1] that kills off several characters, perhaps even Pope Paul V (who historically died in 1621). If Paul dies, the new pope is one of the students' original characters now promoted to pope, not the Gregory XV who historically succeeded. Students assigned to another character who is killed off over the sixteen years are assigned new roles, which could be in different factions with different victory objectives. Not all students will make an easy transition into their new body.

Rivalries has no automatic character death.[2] But it often does have student confusion, because its world deviates from historical reality, sometimes swiftly and significantly. Students on the French team become mystified when France withstands the German attack, unsure what to do next since their historical counterparts offer no guide. US characters usually realize by midsemester that, in their world, the United States is unlikely to engage in any fighting in Europe or East Asia. What do they do now? Japanese admirals are determined to avoid war with the United States. But then what is to be done with all those splendid battleships?

These difficulties are hardly the fault of the students. They have been taught history as an unyielding, fixed time line from grammar school through university. The United States had to win its war for independence. The federal constitution was predestined for ratification. Of course the 1840s were the era of Manifest Destiny, since Henry Clay never had a prayer of being elected president.[3] Sectional differences inevitably led to civil war; nothing could have prevented a Northern victory. And so on. Tests never ask what would have happened if Woodrow Wilson had not been reelected in 1916, or if the United States had joined the League of Nations three years later.

Students cannot comprehend the idea of the past as contingent, as subject to the decisions of individuals, or even serendipity (the 1933 assassination attempt on Roosevelt succeeds, for example). It is as alien to them as the possibility that 1 plus 1 equals 10.[4] From grade through high school, students learn that there is "The Test," and The Test rewards only Right Answers. Their objective is to detect that Right Answer. So it is no surprise that they become lost when *Rivalries*, or any other simulation, ceases to be a scripted reenactment and their decisions actually make a difference.[5] These bewildered souls usually make a beeline to the instructor's office hours, confounded as to how their characters might act in the brave new world they have created collectively.

I address these worries by asking the students to look at their characters as real people who were in the same situation: they had no idea what their future held, either. Has the student accurately captured her or his character's perspective, motives, and goals in their biographical papers (role sheets) they wrote early in the semester? Does a student-Wang recall a similar sense of helplessness in the real one, after he lost control of the Chinese nationalists? The real Stalin secluded himself for a few days after the Nazi invasion, shocked at its scale and success and fearful that all was lost. He was wrong. He had no idea of his future—just like the students of the simulation. Student-Roosevelts are almost universally unhappy when they see no direct US entry into any war. I ask them: in a world like the one the simulation made, how would the real Roosevelt feel? If France defeated Germany, would he have wanted US intervention?

The fact is that it is not just the students' characters that have to cope with the uncertainties of their ever-changing environments, the students themselves, in their real lives, have to cope, too. Some will encounter opportunities. Will they be able to recognize them? Others will suffer setbacks. Can they recover? Student-Churchills will end their semesters marveling at the real Churchill's ability to seize his chance. Student-Lavals or Mussolinis or Wangs, if things turn out historically, will leave the course with newfound respect for their characters who, however flawed, tried to do their best in the face of adversity.

Then again, sometimes there will be students who couldn't care less, students who really are incompetent, lazy, or wrongheaded and become the subject of complaints by other students, usually complaints they direct to the instructor.

Breaking the Sim

Despite the procedures in place in *Rivalries* to avoid subpar student-Hitlers, there will be times when a breezy-to-plain-arrogant student seizes the role and then falls flat on his or her face. Or perhaps they took the role in good faith but had personal problems, family or work commitments, or other course demands that arose. Under such circumstances, other students—especially on the German team—will be frequent office-hour visitors, worried that their evaluations will suffer because Adolf is asleep at the wheel.

Or a student might be altogether too awake in her or his role. At least one student in past *Rivalries*, but usually more, will come into my office asking how his or her team can manage the early acquisition of the atomic bomb, or the assassination of a fellow student, or an instructor-approved way to spy on other teams.

Whatever the source of the problem from the student, it is imperative to keep in mind that only you, the instructor, can break the simulation. The temptation may be great—to replace a failing Hitler, to expedite the Manhattan Project, to give just a little edge to Galileo to ensure that enlightenment has a chance, to make sure that the class ensures votes for women in their *Greenwich Village* reality—but it has to be resisted. The instant you begin adjustments, the simulation stops belonging to the students. They stop learning from it and start looking to you for that Right Answer. Student-Hitler is going to drive Germany into ruin in 1938? Ask the complaining students on the German team whether this was a historical possibility and, if it was, what their characters would have done in response. Galileo loses and his work is lost or ignored? Ask your students whether this ever happened in history, and whether it ever could happen in their own day.

It is vital to keep the students in-character, to keep the simulation intact. In instances when a student thinks otherwise, the instructor's intervention is imperative. Student rebellion is likeliest when said student's team or group is doing poorly. A case in point was one of my German teams. Student-Hitler was an unfortunate mix of high risk and bad judgment. The Third Reich had been conquered and Berlin occupied by the Red Army by 1940. The student representing Hitler happily committed suicide and moved on to a new character. But the student-Himmler, a quick study and excellent learner who had accurately forecast his Germany's sad fate, grimly hung on as Himmler, waging a solitary struggle of resistance against the puppet communist German regime installed by Stalin and a somewhat puzzling willingness of Britain and France to tolerate that regime.

After three weeks of this struggle, student-Himmler disappeared from class. But he surfaced during my office hours to explain that he wanted to drop my course. I pointed out that, while he could do so, university policy would require me to fail him with consequent effect on his grade point average. He was not pleased. He then asked what would happen if he simply resumed attendance but, in effect, sat in a corner glowering at everyone else, especially his erstwhile teammates. I asked him what sort of meaningful journal entries he could make for himself in such a situation. He might not fail the course, but the "A for effort" factor would now count against him, as he would be making no effort. It was not the most pleasant exchange I have had with a student, particularly one who had done good work up to that point. But the student did return to active participation in the simulation.[6]

Instructor Responsibilities

Rules and roles are central. But they are not all. Some simulations require only minimal responsibilities beyond simply ensuring that students stay in role and within outlined procedures. Others require more regular and even vigorous supervision and mediation.

The great majority of simulations virtually run themselves. Your duties as instructor or "gamemaster" are not very different from those of a soccer referee. Blow your whistle to start things off. If play stops, indicate who is to resume it, and how. If there are rule infractions, step in, point them out, and let play resume. Stay out of the way of the players and the ball.

Sometimes a simulation will call for a more active instructor, especially at the start of each class session. *Greenwich Village* suggests brief discussions of the reading assignments at the beginning of earlier sessions to ensure that students are familiar with the context of the assignments. Later, the instructor is responsible for ensuring the orderly scheduling of any public activities, like pageants, parades, or rallies, that various students want to stage. In *Galileo*, the instructor has to determine which characters die between the first and second confrontations between the astronomer and the church and reorder student roles accordingly. The instructor will also score each faction depending upon the eventual rulings of the class's final votes on issues including whether Galileo is guilty of heresy and how his teachings should be handled. *Stages* instructors are closest to referees. So long as rules and decorum are observed, the students call the shots and run the show. One senior (student) member of the queen's Privy Council even handles scheduling matters.

Practically every simulation available, whether from a website or a published text, has a brief Instructor's Manual. But the point is that these manuals are very brief. One of the primary attractions of a simulation, after all, is its ability to put the students not only in roles, but also in charge.

Some simulations, especially longer ones like *Great Power Rivalries*, keep the students in charge, but the very number of student decisions, made in every class, requires a considerable investment of the instructor's time to sort out the interactions among those decisions. In *Rivalries*, there is no final, neat, and decisive vote over suffragist versus labor organizer, or Galileo against the church, or Marlowe versus Shakespeare. Instead, after each and every class session, eight national teams will hand the instructor their turnsheets for the day. Each turnsheet has detailed instructions for that nation's diplomatic, budgetary, and military resources. The instructor has to determine what outcomes result from all of these instructions. Not surprisingly, the instructor's manual for *Rivalries* has a detailed procedure regarding how to resolve these decisions and in exactly what order. Here, clarity is king. The students have to know what is and is not allowed.[7]

For the full monty for this resolution, please contact me. Here, I want to summarize what the instructor's task looks like after each class and explain why the time involved is well spent.

Budget decisions are the simplest. X credits buys Y army or navy or political (Bid) points. Simple transfers on a spreadsheet take care of these in short order.

Diplomacy is trickier. Say it is early in the semester. Students on both the German and French teams have done their homework and realize that a key historical turning point was Germany's uncontested remilitarization of the Rhineland in early 1936. The German team is determined to replicate this success, the students on the French team to reversing it and, they hope, nipping Hitler's dreams for expansion in the bud. Both decide to invest Bid Points in diplomatic actions that are mutually exclusive. Either Germany remilitarizes the Rhineland (by sending German troops into that province), or it cannot, because either France has intimidated Hitler into backing down or, possibly, sending French troops into the province in a repetition of France's 1923 occupation. Here, let's assume the French are especially bold and have opted to attempt a preemptive occupation themselves. Who gets the Rhineland?

The instructor decides, but has to follow a strict set of rules in making the decision—rules that cannot be neatly laid out in a spreadsheet. First, have the French and Germans met any prerequisites for attempting their respective policy attempts? Second, do they have enough cash in their treasuries to execute their attempt? If the answer to either is negative, the attempt will fail and, if the other attempt meets both, it will succeed. If both France and Germany have satisfied all prerequisites and funding, the instructor then has to see which side invested more Bid Points in their attempt. High bid gets to execute its policy. The other fails.

This resolution only takes a few minutes. But remember, there are eight national teams, allowing for plenty of these kinds of resolutions each turn, each class session. For some more complex policies, like the Czech Crisis (which historically took place in late 1938), three or more national teams' decisions might be involved. Those minutes add up, but they are far preferable to a quick but ultimately arbitrary choice by the instructor.

Then there are the military decisions. *Rivalries* must allow for the possibility of war among the powers. These wars cannot be simulated through the detailed, hexagonal maps of traditional war games (well, they could, but maps to rival the Pentagon's war room would be required, and kept in a room on a permanent basis, not very practical in most teaching environments). *Rivalries* uses far simpler maps of provinces to simplify things. France has only six provinces in total, Germany about the same, though the Soviet Union and China have more. Even so, if a Soviet-German war occurs, it can get complicated, with orders easily involving ten or more provinces, sometimes in complex minuets. Resolving these— using a version of rock/paper/scissors tactics selected by the student commanders—will take some time.

When I speak about *Rivalries* at academic conferences with sessions on simulations, my audiences, instructors at secondary schools or colleges, gush initial enthusiasm about the immersive quality of the simulation, gushes that are swiftly extinguished by gasps of horror at the time required to adjudicate student actions after each class session. This adjudication runs only a half hour or so at first, as students themselves learn how the simulation works. But, once they do, even a seasoned instructor will need over an hour to run a set of eight national turnsheets for the day, sometimes longer and on occasion much longer, especially if the adjudication is announced to students in the form of a simulation newspaper (mine is unoriginally titled, *The Daily Planet*) published online the same evening that student actions are resolved.

The Daily Planet
Spring 1938

Sep/Oct:

INITIATIVE

Germany=15+4
Italy=7+3
Britain=5+2
Japan=4+3
USSR=0+2
****
China=0+1
France=X+1
USA=0+0
PRC=0+0

GERMANY DEMANDS SUDETENLAND, SPARKING INTERNATIONAL CRISIS!!!

Frenzied meetings and furious debates characterized the Western response and revealed deep divisions, particularly in France. While London gave every indication of issuing an ultimatum to Berlin, that action was contingent on Paris doing the same. There was strong support there for a parallel measure, but not enough to overcome the united opposition of Bonnet's faction in the Chamber of Deputies, whose members loudly declared that they were not willing to risk "another Verdun" for the sake of Prague.

[French Policy Option (PO) fails due to insufficient Clout Points: 315–115, for a margin in favor of only 200.]

In the absence of Western support, Czech premier Benes saw his country splintered, as local Sudeten Nazis simply took control and announced Germany's annexation of their province. Slovakia seceded. A rump Czech Republic remains, isolated and embittered.

JAPAN CASTIGATES CHINESE BANDIT ACTIVITY!!!

"As occurred in 1931, once again the Chinese nationalists prove unable to control banditry and barbarism within the territory they claim, leaving us no recourse but to restore order there through our own means."

[Japan (JA) has gained casus belli against nationalist China.]

[Please read rules regarding purchase and deployment of garrison points. JA attempt is illegal.]

FROM THE FRONT:

Early blizzards rage across Siberia, spreading unusually wet conditions into western China.

2 Chinese nationalist (CH) Chungking (Pro) v 1 Xibei warlords (XIB) Great Desert (Del) -1 XIB Province falls. War over.

Partisan:
Peking -2 Chinese Communists (CCP)

Nov/Dec:

INITIATIVE

USSR=19+2
Italy=10+3
France=12+1
Britain=5+3
Germany=0+4
****
Japan=0+2
China=0+1
USA=0+0
People's Republic of China (PRC)=0+0

MASSIVE FRENCH COMMUNIST STREET DEMONSTRATIONS INTIMIDATE VOTERS ON CENTER AND RIGHT!!! SOME STREET FIGHTING BETWEEN RED AND RIGHTIST GROUPS!!!

The Third Republic was shaken badly by the waves of Red militants, well organized and in large numbers around every polling place in all major cities and even some of the sleepier towns. Impartial observers noted a significant decrease in voter turnout as a result, although the Reds do not appear to have engaged in ballot box stuffing.

[French Campaign Points depressed for non–French Communist Party (CPF) candidates. See Promise Effects for breakdowns.]

The effort clearly had an effect as the number of CPF deputies rose significantly. In fact, the CPF is now the largest party in that chamber.

[French election succeeds as PO.]

IT'S CIVIL WAR AS YUGOSLAVIA DISSOLVES!!!

Hard on the heels of the Czech breakup, Yugoslavia, another creation of Versailles, has ceased to exist—but on much more bitter terms as fighting has broken out between Serbian forces loyal to the old regime and separatist Croatians, now affiliated with Italy.
[Italy is at war with Serbia. USSR has first right to command Serbian forces.]

FROM THE FRONT:

Clear skies in Europe.

25 Italy (IT) Albania (Pro) v 13 Serbia (SERB) (Spo)
-5 IT -13 SERB
Serbia falls.
Civil war over.
[IT Political Effectiveness increases.]

Partisans:
Peking -2 CCP -4 JA

Taken as an exercise in spreadsheet juggling, the time seems lengthy, even tedious. But in fact the instructor is actually providing feedback and, in the editorial content of *The Daily Planet*, detailed comments on how the students are proceeding. It is fascinating, if a bit perverse, to stare at the click count on the latest posting of *The Daily Planet* and watch it literally light up well into the night as every student checks in and then spreads the word to her or his teammates. To them, the instructor is not just juggling a spreadsheet. They read *The Planet* as commentary on their work, and with considerably greater attention than to most of what any of us might write on their regular class essays or examination booklets. When the next class convenes, many will ask questions, often deep questions, about why the outcome was as it was, and what historical factors they might have missed but can utilize next time. For the instructor, it is an hour's time invested, with dividends that pay for the balance of the semester.

Going Off the Rails

Another way to "break the sim" that may or may not involve students not playing their roles well is the possibility of a veer into fantasy. In a recent

Reacting exchange, an instructor running *The Threshold of Democracy: Athens in 403 BCE*[8] was aghast that his student-characters voted the franchise for women, a possibility not remotely on the horizon in the real Athens of that era. He was advised to impose a strike by dockworkers over the outrageous idea, a step calculated to bring the city to its knees in short order until the vote was withdrawn—then discuss why the dockworkers would have acted as they did.

Seth Offenbach, before he began his semester teaching *Frederick Douglass*, was concerned about the quite clear description in the role sheets of several abolitionists that the connection between the US Constitution and slavery was so umbilical the former had to be torn up to end the latter. He asked: Holy smokes! What if my abolitionists succeed in dismantling the union in 1845? Or, in the *Chicago, 1968*, what if Eugene McCarthy captured the Democratic nomination for president instead of Hubert Humphrey?

My *Rivalries* has dozens of fantastic possibilities. Some students enroll in the simulation because they have seen *The Man in the High Castle* series on Amazon, set in a United States occupied by Nazi and Japanese forces after their victory in World War II. That alternative world never happened in any of my simulations. But in quite a few, Germany does conquer the Soviet Union and forces peace upon a diminished Britain. In one, Germany persuaded France, Britain, and the United States to adopt Nazi-like laws. France has defeated a German invasion a number of times. Japan rarely attacks the United States, but often ends up dominating Chinese or even Soviet territories in East Asia. How much should the instructor tolerate? When should she step in (as in the *Athens* simulation) and put things back on track?

Almost never. Because simulations are not reenactments, because they may veer off in different directions, a cardinal rule for the instructor is not to play the Almighty. Let the chips fall where they may. But if things really go in quite implausible directions, the instructor needs to find creative—and historically plausible—ways to get things back on track.

The key term here is "plausible." For example, suppose you begin the *Galileo* simulation in a general education course that has students from a wide variety of majors. Suppose some of them are science or engineering majors, assigned to be rigid churchmen, and suppose they simply rebel, asserting that, whatever the simulation materials say and whatever their roles dictate, the students simply cannot bring themselves to imagine Galileo to be in error. To them, it is a simple case of dogma against empirical knowledge and they will not adopt or adapt to their roles.

Hopefully this problem will emerge before the simulation's final session and vote on Galileo's fate. Once it does, the instructor will have to intervene. Step one should be to remind the students of their core responsibility in a simulation: to understand, respect, and represent their roles regardless. If this effort fails, it is time to switch roles, perhaps by having a plague roll through, allowing role reassignments with a degree of historical plausibility. If role shifts are not enough, it may be necessary to give additional weight to the votes of the conservative churchmen, and justify that weight with historically sound explanations.

But, as a rule, things should be allowed to play out, even if some students are discomfited. In *Great Power Rivalries*, it is possible that Nazi Germany will conquer the Soviet Union, or vice versa. Students on the losing side will be unhappy, especially if they lose with a good deal of the simulation (and therefore semester) to go. What are they to do during class, with no country, no income, no military, and nothing to fill in on their turnsheets?

In these situations, the instructor must first apply the test of historical plausibility. Could the Nazis have conquered the Soviets? Could the Soviets have conquered the Nazis? We know that the latter is not only plausible, it happened. Most historians would not rule out the possibility that Stalin's regime might have collapsed, and with it the Soviet Union. So, the plausibility test will not save the hapless students on the losing team.

That same test suggests how the students should continue. Yes, the Nazi government was shattered in 1945. But Germany went on. So should the students. The instructor should offer each student options, albeit plausible ones. Student-Hitler might have to select among turning himself over to the Soviet authorities (doubtless for a show trial, which ought to be held in the simulation, with all students invited to participate or observe), committing suicide (and returning to the simulation as a brand new character), or trying to go underground to lead a desperate Nazi resistance against the occupiers (perhaps in hopes of igniting a war between the Soviets and the West that will offer room for his eventual return to power). Similar options can be offered to losing Soviets or, as often happens, to students on the French team that find themselves treading the path of actual historical events all too accurately. Likewise, what if the abolition-ists in *Frederick Douglass* do somehow rip up the Constitution in 1845? It might be a salutary, and fascinating, not so fantastic, way to explore what might happen next. Reality is contingent. Good simulations should be too.

The Student Who Would Not Speak

The great majority of students enjoy simulations and avidly participate in them. A minority find active participation difficult. This situation is hardly unique to simulations. Many courses require participation or discussion as a component or percentage of the student's overall evaluation as a way to encourage valuable career and social skills such as public speaking, advocacy, and group conversation. No matter what incentives are pro-vided, some students will balk.

Some instructors compensate for these students by providing them with alternative ways of satisfying course requirements. A student who does not or cannot join in classroom discussion and debate might be offered extra credit in the form of a supplemental written assignment, for example. In a simulation, such a student could be given a nonspeak-ing role, perhaps composing and handing out pamphlets for the suf-fragists in *Greenwich Village*, or providing a background briefing paper on a scientific or theological issue in *Galileo*, or being assigned a quiet, deliberative role in *Stages* instead of one requiring presentation or actual performance.

While there is nothing wrong with these approaches, it is worth remem-bering that simulations offer a different way of addressing of student shy-ness. Remind students that, once they step into the simulation, they are not themselves any more. They are their characters, characters who nearly always will be bolder, more assertive types—which is why their actual per-sons became historically noteworthy. Sam Bashful the student has become Edward Alleyn of Marlowe's "Lord Admiral's Men" stage company. Sam might be afraid of speaking a word in public, but Edward has played the world-conquering Tamburlaine the Great in Marlowe's play of the same name.[9]

The Simulation That Would Not End

History doesn't end; simulations do. This part of history, of reality, cannot be adequately simulated. Most simulations finesse the issue by orchestrating fixed endings that provide some resolution to the central issues the simulation is addressing. *Stages* has its final vote of the Privy Council, *Galileo* its church tribunal. *Greenwich Village* climaxes with its characters supporting the IWW demonstration or suffragist march (or possible alternative outcomes). This finesse is imperative. The simulation cannot continue forever. More to the point, the students know when the decisive day will arrive, and pitch all their efforts toward winning that decision. The instructor will pay special attention to the finale's proceedings.

Great Power Rivalries takes a different approach. Even though it runs much longer than most simulations, it cannot run past the academic semester, so students, unlike their characters, can anticipate a final turn. The temptation to risk all or much on a last throw of the dice is great. It is also contrary to the spirit of the simulation. The historical Hitler may have opted for Germany's Götterdämmerung, but he was not able to affect its timing. Emperor Hirohito did force a Japanese surrender much earlier than the Imperial Army preferred, but Allied power, not his, enabled his intervention to throw in the towel. More crucially, history went on afterward. How can a simulation replicate the continuity of history when everyone knows it, and its class, must end with the semester?

True replication is impossible, needless to say. But it is not difficult to discourage the students from taking final session risks, secure in the knowledge that if their bet turns toward disaster, they will be saved by the end of classes. I never tell the students exactly which day will be the last of *Rivalries*, because I do not know myself. About two weeks before the end of the semester, I figuratively roll my own dice after each class,[10] with the odds of the result ending the simulation increasing each time. There is no need to deceive the students or withhold information from them. As important, no student will have grounds for feeling unequally or unfairly treated. Sometimes, the instructor's mightiest power is to deprive her- or himself the ability to decide or dictate.

Debriefing and Reflection

History does not end, but simulations do. One of the most valuable parts of any classroom simulation is its postmortem: dedicated class sessions where students reflect on what happened, why it happened, and what part they played in both the what and the why. These meetings often are just as animated as the simulation sessions. They ought to be an indispensable part of the overall exercise.

Students usually approach these postmortems defensively. They are reluctant to depart from their roles, whether they, in those roles, did well in the simulation or not. Students representing the church or the scientist in *Galileo* will insist that their perspectives had validity and deserve respect. Proponents of Marlowe and Shakespeare will maintain that their plays and production deserved performance in *Stages*. Neither unionist nor suffragist will disavow the worth of their causes in *Greenwich Village*.

Great Power Rivalries is no different. I ask each national team to present an "after-action report" to the class as a whole, leaving to it the details of which team members should talk, for how long, and about what. Almost always, these reports focus on the actions of that team, or a student-character on it, that dramatically influenced the course of the simulation. Why Germany decided to attack the Soviet Union first instead of France, for example. Or why Britain refused to support a France ready for war during the simulation's Czech crisis.

Students are eager to tell their stories. But it is just as important to allow time for them to field questions from their peers. These questions lead to students understanding the different perspectives that other students in other roles had. They also allow students to see events as a historian does—from many perspectives.

Every simulation benefits from a postmortem. If *Greenwich Village* ends with a conclusive victory for the suffragists, the students might ask if contemporary concerns made them more sensitive to the arguments of women. Or they might be asked if any of them could remember actually seeing a labor strike in their real lives. Why have women's issues dominated headlines in recent years, but workers' issues have not?

Similar lines might be explored after *Galileo* concludes. Once students representing conservative church leaders shed their vestments, they can venture (confess?) that they actually thought their characters to be stuffed-shirted, antiscience bigots who blindly stood in the way of the advance of knowledge. Do these students see similar manifestations today? Can they use their study of their characters to give them insights into those manifestations and contemporary adherents? Are contemporary bigots simply bigots, or are they honest believers in a different world view, much as those churchmen were? Or the pro-Galileans might be asked whether scientists today have become a bit stuffy in the shirt themselves, intolerant and dismissive of any opinions on subjects they regard as within the scientific realm and therefore subject only to scientific rules of evidence and judgment.

One object common to all postmortems is to ask students if they questioned their characters' basic assumptions—and whether they have learned to question their own such assumptions. For many, this can be a profound examination extremely difficult to achieve in conventional courses. Mark Carnes recounts a story of a student, devoutly Christian, who enrolled in a course on the Old Testament at California State University at Long Beach. Its conventional aspects were unremarkable. Then its students began a simulation on *The Josianic Reform: Deuteronomy, Prophecy, and Israelite Religion*. The simulation takes place in the Jerusalem of 622 BCE, focusing on debates over the inclusion of the Book of Deuteronomy in what would become the Bible. The student had a role requiring her to argue that Deuteronomy was indeed the Word of God, but the more deeply she researched her character's background and arguments, the more troubled she became. Was it possible to doubt? To wonder if all-too-human factors had become entangled in the debates of 622 and had influenced what turned out to be an all-too-human decision? Afterward, the student remained a deep and sincere Christian, but one who had learned to read the Bible and her faith in a radically new way.[11]

Rivalries has not produced any reaffirmations of Nazism. But my most recent postmortem did lead to an animated discussion of whether people in the United States today joining the alt-right did so for reasons or motivations comparable to Nazi supporters of the 1930s. Facile dismissals were not much in evidence. Students debated whether both phenomena were primarily top-down, driven by charismatic leaders with strongly articulated views, or bottom-up, broad-based movements fueled by deep concerns over the future of oneself and one's country.

Students also used the postmortem to argue how *Rivalries* had led them to see the Soviet Union's position in the Cold War, and perhaps even the Russian Federation's position today, in a new light. Germany's early collapse in one of my simulations sent students running to study how the Federal Republic had been created from the ruins. They learned that building a new state from the carcass of an old one is a good deal harder than it looks.

As all these cases illustrate, classroom simulations are especially good at forcing students to deep-dive into the past. It is not enough to say that church officials followed doctrine in the time of Galileo. The troupers of Marlowe and Shakespeare had to have an acute and sensitive appreciation of lèse majesté. Students have to think hard about how the Bible came to be what it was 1,500 years ago. A good simulation, and a good postmortem, give them a great opportunity to reflect on what they have learned.

7

UNDER THE HOOD

A central objective of any simulation, as with any class session, is keeping the students focused on that session's activity—listening to a lecture, participating in discussion, or playing a role in a simulation. Ideally, every student will pay rapt attention to the lecture. Discussion participation will be universal. Ideally, there would be a disease-free world peace too.

Having a few students watching YouTube does not detract from the others' ability to listen to a lecture. It is fine if those dedicated half dozen always carry a discussion forward during recitations while everyone else dozes. But a simulation demands that everyone take part and be their character, all the time. A clump of passive observers or, worse, a group that refuses to "play along," will dampen the effectiveness of the simulation for all. As the previous chapter noted, sometimes the instructor has to persuade or coerce a passive or resistant student to take part. But this can get old quickly, especially if the dropouts start to multiply.

Accordingly, a good simulation will be designed to offer interesting activities for every participant for every class session. There are a number of ways to achieve such a goal. *Galileo* mandates a specific set of activities for each class session. Its fourth class session, for example, requires lectures by four Jesuits, each from a specific faction, and interpellation by a presiding professor. Other student-characters then join in discussion and rebuttal. Both *Stages* and *Greenwich Village* have a looser structure. All sessions build toward the final, decisive class meeting, but the earlier ones can be strategy sessions for the rival companies (Shakespeare and Marlowe) or factions (laborers or suffragists) or even more informal commingling to garner allies or Influence Points.

Rivalries has both less and more structure for each class, but a format geared directly toward keeping every student involved all the time. To explain, let's take a look under its hood, at how the mechanics of the simulation make the students run it. In other words, how the structure of the simulation compels students to be active in every class session.

Startup

Whenever I learn a new game, or want to explain one to someone new to it, I begin with its sequence of play. In what order do things happen? Or, to put it from the student's point of view: what am I supposed to do first?

On its surface, *Rivalries* could not be simpler. At the start of class, each national team receives a plastic file folder. Inside is a turnsheet and the latest copy of the simulation newsletter, *The Daily Planet*, summarizing the outcomes of the last session. During class, each team will conduct internal discussions and debates as well as negotiations with other teams to determine what actions it will attempt on its turnsheet for that class. For the democracies of Britain, France, and the United States, if there is an election due, the students on those teams must submit their individual campaign decisions as well. At the end of class, I collect the folders with the completed turnsheets (and possibly election campaign decisions), run the turns, and compose the next issue of *The Daily Planet* which will be handed out at the start of the next class (and posted online the night before class).

Obviously, the first class of the semester will not have a *Planet* composed from my write-up of what the students attempted in their turn-sheets. I use a kickoff issue that can be seen in the text box.[1]

The Daily Planet
January 1936

Initiative:

Italy=?+4
Germany=?+3
France=?+3
Japan=?+2
Britain=?+2
USSR=?+1
China=?+1
USA=?+0

**ITALIAN ONSLAUGHT
CONTINUES IN AFRICA!**

Mussolini's legions continue their advance toward Addis Ababa, despite howls of protest from Paris and London, howls that seem rather barren given recently broken stories of a proposed deal from the democracies to Italy. When asked if he was concerned about the League of Nations, Il Duce replied, "They are a bunch of sheep, and I am hungry for mutton!"

**PRIME MINISTER BALDWIN
CARRIES ON**

Stanley Baldwin continued his unflappable ways, refusing to let the roiling international situation disturb his tea or, for that matter, his vacation schedules. "Good tours are hard to book and I shan't lose what opportunities I have to enjoy them," he said.

LAVAL TEETERS IN FRANCE!

It seems nearly certain that Pierre Laval's ministry will collapse quite soon, but it is not at all clear what sort of French regime will follow. Noted intellectual Jean-Paul Sartre has been praising Leon Blum and his Popular Front, but when asked if he intended to vote, replied, "I cannot be bothered with such a trivial activity."

**HITLER DECLARES NEW
YEAR TO BE "BEST YET"**

As he prepared to celebrate the third anniversary of his becoming Reichskanzler, Adolf Hitler made his boldest assurances yet that the new year would see Germany reach still greater heights. Whatever could he have in mind?

AMERICAN TELEPHONE POLLING SHOWS FDR WELL BEHIND IN UPCOMING REELECTION BID!

Despite an economic slump of numbing intensity, the Yanks are bound by their constitution to hold a vote this coming autumn. A new political development, "polling," in which "pollsters" contact prospective voters by phone to ask which way they intend to vote, shows nearly any Republican hopeful with a commanding lead. But of course, time shall tell.

CHINESE CHAOS CONTINUES!

A delicate ceasefire between nationalist and communist forces still holds as some local warlords demand action against the Japanese.

Some of these articles are just for flavor. Hitler feels confident. Baldwin is set on his vacation. But most either report facts or offer hints at what might be upcoming or both. The Italian team is reminded that they start the semester at war with Ethiopia and will have to figure out the simulation's land combat procedures right away. France will need to hold elections soon and it looks like anyone can win. The United States will have its own presidential contest. The US team will have to master that election procedure straightaway. The Chinese characters are informed that their civil war is on hold for the moment, if they wish to keep things that way.

Then there is the somewhat mysterious Initiative section. Why all those numbers, not to mention the sea of question marks? Initiative determines the order in which I process the national teams' turnsheets. As such, it is a crucial, often decisive, component of the simulation.

Initiative is determined by a simple sum for each national team: the number of Bid Points it invests on behalf of the Policy Option(s) it wishes to pursue that turn, plus a "momentum" constant that reflects the team's prior Initiative ranking. The team ranked first after the last class session receives four momentum points for the current one, second and third teams get three each, and so on.

Why is Initiative ranking often decisive? To illustrate: suppose Germany is eager to reoccupy the Rhineland (one of Germany's Policy Options) and invests eight Bid Points from its Bid Point pool (tracked on a spreadsheet) toward that end. France has a Policy Option to preemptively occupy the Rhineland itself and the French team's turnsheet invests five Bid Points for that option. Meanwhile, Italy has decided to invest two Bid Points trying for an economic agreement with a minor power, Poland. The Soviet Union is going for the same thing, throwing four of its Bid Points into the effort. The other great powers have elected not to attempt any Policy Options and are spending nothing from their Bid Point pools.

These decisions would result in the following Initiative order:

Germany=8+3
France=5+3
Italy=2+4
USSR=4+1
Japan=0+2
Britain=0+2
China=0+1
USA=0+0

It is not just ranking in this list that determined which Policy Options will be attempted; *Great Power Rivalries* also has a screen for determining the total number of attempts possible on any given turn. In brief, this number varies using a procedure seeded by a random number.[2] One Policy Option will always be attempted per turn. Eight Policy Options almost never will be. Typically, between three and six options will be possible on any given turn. Let's assume that, for our sample turn, four are possible.

Germany goes first. Assuming Germany has met the prerequisites of the Rhineland Policy Option, that option will succeed and France is out of luck. Germany won the race. France's Bid Points are lost in a futile attempt. Italy is going to be able to go for that economic agreement with Poland, and only if the Poles refuse (a procedure governed by Poland's diplomatic position as a minor power, also tracked on a spreadsheet) will the Soviets be able to have a shot (which Poland will almost certainly refuse, as Poland at the start of the simulation is quite unfriendly toward the Soviet Union). Regardless of who wins or loses, who can try an attempt and who is unlucky with the random seed, all Bid Points invested are expended. They will have to be replenished by purchasing them using credits (or dollars or simbucks or whatever term you wish to employ) from the nation's treasury.

Money

Simulations require constrained resources, whether it is the number of votes to be cast to determine Galileo's fate, the number of bodies in Greenwich Village's final marches, or the amount of cash in a nation's budget in *Rivalries*. There, nations have income that contributes to a pool of credits. They can spend those credits for points of various sorts.[3] Students quickly learn what they must do to increase their income. They are generally much slower to figure out the most effective spending strategies. (Just like real life!)

Income per turn is calculated by using the lower of two numbers. One is the total number of "resources" controlled by a nation. These resources are fixed and appear in provinces around the world. They abstractly represent mineral deposits of coal, iron ore, copper, and so forth as well as one special class of resource with effects beyond simply counting toward national income, namely oil. If a nation controls six resources, its income per turn may never rise above six.

But that income might be below six. The other number used to calculate income is somewhat more flexible. Each nation has a number of factories, also in provinces it controls. The total number of factories is multiplied by a "Production Multiple" to determine the second ceiling on a nation's possible production. If a nation controls ten factories, for example, and its Production Multiple is 0.3, then the factory ceiling on its national income would be three. If that nation had six resources, then, the lower of the resource ceiling (6) and factory ceiling (3) would determine its income per turn, which here would be three.

National income can be increased or decreased. The resource ceiling can be raised by obtaining control of additional provinces with resources. That control can be a straightforward military conquest of the province, or it might be secured by an economic agreement with the minor power that owns such a province. Or, a minor country might decide to grant your nation control of its resources, perhaps even its army, if you court it sufficiently well through diplomacy or intimidate it through other Policy Options available to you. Of course, if another power seizes a resource province you had controlled, by military or other means, your resource ceiling will decline.

Factory ceilings are not quite such a zero-sum game, though no nation will want to ever lose provinces with factories. It is possible, though quite expensive, to build a factory in one of a nation's home provinces. More often, nations will strive to increase their Production Multiple, an abstract but effective way to simulate the diversion of regular, peacetime factory capacity to more potentially militant purposes. This production increase is accomplished by successfully attempting a specific Policy Option (customarily named "Gear Up for War"), which of course requires the clever use of Bid Points. To continue the example above, if a nation with ten factories successfully "geared up" and increased its Production Multiple from 0.3 to 0.5, its production ceiling would increase from three to five, as would its income per turn (provided it still controlled six resources).

Every nation, if it could, would try to "gear up" every possible turn, so as to increase its income steadily and significantly. In practice, doing so is quite difficult. There is a host of restraining factors in *Great Power Rivalries*. The "gear up" Policy Options themselves carry restrictive prerequisites. Sometimes these are chronological—a given attempt may not be made until 1938, for example. Sometimes they are conditional. France may not attempt to gear up a second time until Germany has done so, for instance. Or the United States might not be able to attempt a "gear up" at all until it is at war with another major power. Beyond these prerequisites, each "gear up" option carries a fixed cost in credits, and these costs increase as subsequent gear-ups are attempted. Last but hardly least, if many nations are attempting gear-ups on the same turn, only those who have also invested Bid Points sufficient to literally outbid their competitors will have a chance for success.

Credits will be hard to come by, so spending wisely becomes crucial for a national team's prospects. No simulation, even a relatively intricate one, can hope to approach the complexity of historical budgetary decision-making. But any simulation worth its salt will attempt to come as close as possible to that complexity. In *Great Power Rivalries*, credits can be used to buy: Bid Points, vital if a nation wants its Policy Options to have any chance of success; Army Points, necessary to take and hold provinces;

Fleet Points, useful in asserting control over sea provinces; Escort Points, equivalent to both merchant shipping and the light warships that protect or escort them, economically essential to island powers like Britain or Japan, but also useful for transporting Army Points across water; and Submarine Points, which seek to destroy Escort Points. Credits are also essential to pay for most Policy Options once they have successfully been attempted. Budget spending decisions alone can keep every member of every team busy for the entire class.

Conflict

Nearly every simulation involves conflict. The suffragists and laborers of *Greenwich Village* might all favor social reform, but ultimately one or the other will be more successful recruiting for their cause. *Stages* will see Marlowe or Shakespeare performed, not both. *Galileo* and its trial will yield a verdict.

Rivalries' approach might not. Unlike most simulations, which orchestrate a final vote or decision, *Rivalries* does not mandate any wars. It does not mandate anything, for that matter, though it does inform the students of the Nazi team that their performance will not go well unless they take steps to resolve the Jewish Problem, as true Nazis should. Otherwise, there is no encouragement or direction for students except to play their roles as accurately and effectively as they can. In the terminology of simulations, *Rivalries* is a "sandbox" game. The players have wide latitude in determining their actions. They write the script themselves.

For instructors, this can be unnerving because they are not in control. Ceding control to the students, however, is the essence of how simulations engage them. Even the shorter simulations do so to a considerable extent. Sometimes the *Greenwich Village* suffragists will get the most participation, sometimes they won't. *Galileo* will be found guilty of heresy in some classes, in others he will not. Shakespeare or Marlowe? *Stages* can go either way.

Rivalries can go any which way. But if that is true, what prevents students from travelling into highly improbable territory, such as war between Britain and the United States, or a combination of Japan and the Chinese communists against the Soviet Union? What stops the whole simulation from running off the rails of historical plausibility?

The most fundamental check against such a possibility is the most fundamental element of any simulation: the roles. Would Mao Zedong have taken up arms against Stalin under any circumstances, let alone alongside the Japanese? Winston Churchill may have been virtually alone in hoping that the United States would help Britain, but there was no one in London contemplating war against them under the remotest circumstances. There was plenty of anti-British sentiment in many corners of the United States, from populists in the Mississippi valley to Irish American bastions in the cities, but none of these thought war the answer to Britain's past or perceived sins. *Rivalries'* only near mandate, in fact, is just a reminder to the Nazis to play their roles accurately.

The second powerful restraint against unreality comes in the form of Policy Options open to the various national teams. While each has a wide variety to choose from,[4] those options themselves fall within the realm of the plausible and possible. For example, only Britain and the United States may develop heavy bombers capable of inflicting direct damage on an enemy's production, because only those two nations maintained strategic bomber programs through the 1920s and 1930s. Britain, Germany, and the United States may pursue atomic weapons research, and the Soviet Union may enter the race with the assistance of espionage operations once any of the first three are well along in their development, but China simply has no ability to attempt it. Stalin can order communist street demonstrations anywhere he likes, but their impact will be nil in nations with scant Red presence. Franklin Roosevelt cannot declare war against anyone. He needs enough votes in Congress to do so, and the path to those votes is paved (or mined) with many Policy Option prerequisites.

Because Policy Options serve to keep things plausible, they have to be written with an eye to historical reality. But since a simulation is not a rote reenactment, those options have to allow historical alternatives to be explored. Sometimes this requires thought about what might have been. One Policy Option open to Germany raises a darker possibility about the abdication of Edward VIII in 1937. It reads:

GE-21: TURN KING EDWARD VIII
Prereq: Must not be or have been at war with Britain.
Cost: $3

Effects: Britain cannot have a better Initiative ranking than Germany. If the British expend Bid Points so as to achieve a better ranking, these expenditures are automatically voided.

Historically, the public reason given for Edward's abdication was his desire to marry a US divorcée. But there was always a whiff of his sympathies for, or at least his resignation to the power of, the German Nazis. It seems reasonable to give students on the German team an interest in examining Edward and, if they exercise GE-21, compel students on the British team to confront the possibility of forcing Edward's abdication or tolerating the public distractions that his actions historically created.

Sometimes the simulation bends history a bit to give students choice rather than imposing a historical script on them. To use another example: should the simulation simply decree that a civil war has broken out in Spain in July 1936? There is no question about that war's domestic origins, but there should be a question about whether it or its timing should be imposed upon students in the earliest sessions of the simulation, especially given its potentially decisive impact upon the wider situation in Europe. To me, instead of imposition by instructor's fiat, it seemed reasonable to encourage students to research the Spanish civil war by giving them the option of triggering it. The logical national team to give this option to was Italy. Hence an Italian Policy Option:

IT-37A: SPANISH CIVIL WAR
Prereq: None.
Cost: variable: if 1936: 2; if 1937: 5; if 1938 or later: 10
Effect: Spanish civil war commences. For this round only, Italy may spend an additional $1 for one Army Point or $2 for two Army Points for the fascist side.

Italy can start the Spanish civil war if it likes, when it likes, and can get a jump in aiding Franco's fascists if it does. Italy has similar Policy Options to kick off civil wars in Yugoslavia or Greece.

Giving the students on the Italian team the option of triggering these wars is not strictly historical, but it is not implausible, either. More to the point, it encourages those students to study those wars to determine if, in the actual historical time line, they developed or could have developed to Italy's advantage. In both of these examples, the objective is not to give

Germany or Italy an advantage in the simulation, it is to spur interest in learning about history, even if a by-product might be such an advantage. Good students, in fact, will eagerly read all they can about their characters and countries to try to gain insights into history and, with them, edges in the simulation. Their choices will determine how closely, or distantly, their simulation's world adheres to the historical one.

Quite often, those choices lead to a world decisively different from reality. Far from failing to teach history, postsimulation reflection on the differences leads to deeper realization of why the real world turned out as it did. *Rivalries* results in counterfactual history, but of a kind that does force new consideration of the past as it actually unfolded.

My famous example is the day of infamy that almost never happens in the simulation. In *Great Power Rivalries*, Japan just does not attack the United States. Other variables have no effect on this outcome, or lack thereof. It does not matter if Germany is succeeding even more than Hitler's actually did, or is doing far worse. The disposition of forces, political and military, on the Asian mainland makes no difference whatsoever. Ensuring that the Dutch East Indies has enough oil to end any of Tokyo's worries about energy scarcity does not tempt members of the Japanese team. Even stretching the simulation's rules regarding fleet combat, a stretching that makes a simulated Pearl Harbor even more devastating than the actual one, does not move the students representing Japan one jot toward even considering military operations against the United States.

One might conclude that this is simply an instance of 20–20 hindsight at work. Today's students cannot conceive of a world in which the United States is not dominant militarily. They are well aware that Japan's actual attack on Hawaii ended with two of their cities in atomic ashes. They simply wish to avoid such a fate, albeit a simulated one.

But that is just my point. My students have nothing to lose but their course grades, and not even those, if they make a good case for their decisions in their simulation journals. The actual Japanese leaders may not have seen Hiroshima coming, but they were aware of the considerable risk involved in bringing the United States into a war that already had denied them easy victory over the Chinese and a series of costly border encounters with the Soviet Red Army. The actual Japanese leaders were literally risking their real lives. Many of them and millions of their countrymen paid with those lives. Why did they take that chance?

Answering this question compels the students to look at the historical record more closely and examine their own decisions in the simulation from that perspective. When they do—and they usually do from the beginning of the simulation, not its end—they understand that the decision to attack Pearl Harbor was far from a bilateral United States–Japanese affair. It stemmed from Japan's inability to force the Chinese nationalists to sue for peace and a hope that shutting off China's last lines to the West via French Indochina and British Burma would compel such a suit. It stemmed from the Japanese army's great hope that Germany's crushing initial attack on the Soviet Union would allow a quick and decisive blow against the Soviets in East Asia. It stemmed from a belief that Nazi victory over Russia would compel Britain to stand down, and in turn a United States, faced with the prospect of no allies to fight alongside and a long, transoceanic war if it fought alone, would recognize new realities and be content in the Western hemisphere.

It is true that much had to go right for Japan to make this appealing vision come true. But in the actual summer of 1941 everything appeared to be going right. The likeliest Japanese preference that season was to attack the Soviet Union, occupy the European colonies, and starve out China. The crucial flaw to these arrangements, as is well known, was the US decision to freeze Japanese assets, thereby denying Japan oil imports from the United States necessary to literally fuel an attack on the Soviets.[5] The Japanese army reluctantly agreed to an attack on the Dutch East Indies to get the oil necessary for such an eventual attack, and the Japanese navy insisted that taking the Indies was fruitless unless the US fleet was neutralized, thus Pearl Harbor.

Armed with this insight, most Japanese teams will strive to avoid war in China, and most simulations see a Japanese attack on the Soviet Union, nearly always in combination with Germany. There is nothing illogical or, for that matter, really counterfactual in such a strategy. The real interest, I would argue, is that actual history itself was rather illogical. But whether that is true or not, the fact remains that the what-ifs of a simulation encourage students to look beneath the what-happened and try to figure out the why-it-happened, if only to avoid the errors of their historical counterparts. The "sandbox" of the simulation leads directly to questioning how much unalterable bedrock is at the foundation of the history we know.

By the same token, "sandbox" simulations need to be constructed every bit as carefully as those with mandated or fixed class sessions. They have to prevent wildly implausible developments. But they also, like all simulations, have to ensure that every student has something interesting to do during every class session. That is what makes that engine under the hood run.

8

SIMULATIONS FOR AN AFTERNOON

If you have gotten this far, you must still be interested in the possibilities of using simulations in your classroom. But perhaps you are not ready for the semester-long foray that *Great Power Rivalries* needs, or still a bit wary about committing even a week or two of class time to one of the briefer simulations discussed here or available from the Reacting to the Past websites or elsewhere. If so, this chapter is for you. It describes simulations that I have run with great success that last for a single class session (sometimes two). Each such simulation is brief, but that brevity sacrifices none of the important elements or advantages of a classroom simulation.

An afternoon's simulation allows no time for character study, classroom speeches, or protracted negotiations. To properly simulate the need for speed, the subject matter should be set in a time of crisis, requiring rapid decisions with immediate consequences. Luckily, history is replete with such crises, from plagues[1] to wars. Three that I have run are *Guns of August*, simulating the frenzied international deliberations that led to the outbreak of the First World War; *Japan: 1941*, a look at critical decisions in Tokyo that year that plunged Japan and the United States into the Second World War; and *Missiles of October*, the Cuban Missile Crisis of 1962, that could have led to a Third.[2]

Missiles in Cuba

For a microsimulation, a concise but thorough role sheet for each student is imperative. Students will have no time to consult in-depth sources themselves, so a layout of their character's positions, powers, and goals is essential. What they can do and what they should try to be doing should be crystal clear. Even things that might seem obvious need to be spelled out. President Kennedy's sheet, for example, must note that he is acutely aware of Republican attacks on him, as a Democrat, as soft on communism, and that he had striven mightily to dispel that impression among the US public. It needs to note Kennedy's feeling that he was much outmatched by his counterpart from the Soviet Union, Nikita Khrushchev, at their summit conference in Vienna a year earlier. But it also should point out that Kennedy is aware that the United States holds a significant superiority in nuclear weapons, yet the utility of that superiority has been challenged by the United States' European allies, who are fearful that, in any confrontation, the United States will not risk a general nuclear exchange that might kill millions of its own citizens, preferring some compromise that would be at Europe's expense.

The variables and factors raised in Kennedy's role sheet can be reinforced by other students' roles themselves. For example, a student might take the role of Ted Sorenson, a Kennedy speechwriter keenly attuned to the domestic political implications of anything the president might do. Another could be General Curtis LeMay of the Strategic Air Command, ready (and eager) to blast the communists at any opportunity. LeMay's role sheet should equip him with ready-made and historically accurate military options that he can present to Kennedy. Yet another student (or students) could play European ambassadors to Washington, with easy access to Kennedy but uneasy feelings about what he might do. Their role sheets must make clear that if the US does go for a military resolution to Soviet missiles in Cuba, the resulting wider conflict is likely to incinerate their cities, not Washington or New York. If numbers allow, it is useful to have one or more students represent hard-line (usually Republican) members of Congress, always ready to confirm that Kennedy indeed is soft on the Reds.

Matters should be similarly complex and conflicted on the Soviet side. Khrushchev might be a tough talker, but he knows that the United States has called his nuclear missile bluff. At the start of the crisis, the Soviets have no intercontinental ballistic missile (ICBM) force of note while the United States is building plenty in addition to their submarine-based missiles and shorter-range land-based ones located in Western Europe, Turkey, and the Pacific. The Soviet Red Army is demanding huge expenditures to forge a real ICBM force and, in the meantime, would like to quickly increase Soviet capabilities to threaten the US homeland by placing shorter-range (and much cheaper) Soviet missiles in Cuba.

Soviet missiles in Cuba seem attractive to a second group of Soviet leaders. The Soviet economy is not robust, and some Soviet economic experts think a fresh arms race unwise over both short and long terms. For them, missiles in Cuba represent an acceptably cheap fix over the long term, so long as frictions with the United States can be averted. Better to spend more on agriculture and infrastructure to render the economy stronger in the future.

The Cuban Missile Crisis was also Cuban—a third team in the simulation. Fidel Castro takes pride in his country's repulse of an US-backed invasion attempt at the Bay of Pigs a year earlier, but remains deeply concerned that the Yanquis will try again, this time with their own marines and air force. He wants a wide range of Soviet aid: Soviet ground forces (perhaps augmented with tactical or battlefield nuclear charges) to help repel the US assault; Soviet surface-to-air missiles capable of shooting down the high-flying US U-2 spy planes that regularly violate Cuban airspace; Soviet jet fighters that can give lower-level US reconnaissance and armed warplanes real opposition; and perhaps even some Soviet nuclear ballistic missiles, to give the United States something to think about before they even try to land. Castro and his advisers (perhaps including Che Guevara, if you feel frisky) are to act as gadflies, urging Moscow to ever stronger actions, but they are gadflies with real reasons to worry about their future, and any arrangements the Soviets and the United States might make at their expense.

For a brief simulation that can be run in a single session, roles have to be absolutely clear and friction points must be swiftly reached.[3] This constellation of three teams and anywhere from ten to thirty roles guarantees a good amount of friction and hence difficult decisions. The rules of the simulation can be short, simply outlining what possibilities are open to selection. For example, for the United States, a single page is sufficient:

The USA's toolbox:
The USA has a wide variety of steps available. Some of these are:

INTELLIGENCE AND DIPLOMACY:

The CIA can increase its periodic overflights of Cuba or the USSR in its U-2s. Bear in mind that the USSR has demonstrated its ability to shoot these down.

While there are no moles inside the Kremlin, the tried-and-true intel source of the US ambassador's office is available for the USSR. The US has no diplomats in Cuba.

You can always request to talk with the USSR's ambassador in Washington.

For Cuba, you have loads of refugees in Florida to talk to.

MILITARY: AIR

Low-level air reconnaissance will give you much better information for Cuba.

This reconnaissance may be designated "armed," meaning planes are authorized to use force if fired upon.

You may actively suppress Soviet or Cuban surface-to-air missiles (SAMs) or antiaircraft facilities to ease the task of your recon aircraft.

You may bomb those facilities outright.

If proper DEFCON is reached, you may initiate similar measures directly against the USSR using bombers, IRBM's based in Europe, or ICBM's from the US mainland.

MILITARY: SEA

Search and seize Soviet ships bound for Cuba.

Actively locate (use active SONAR on) Soviet submarines in the West Atlantic and Caribbean. (This cannot be hidden from the Soviets.)

Destroy those submarines.

Assist in an amphibious invasion of Cuba.

MILITARY: LAND

US forces in Europe follow DEFCON restrictions and allowances.
Reserves may be called up.
The US Marine Corps has a small invasion-ready force that may be used at will.
A larger invasion of Cuba, requiring US Army forces, will require time.

For the Soviets:

The USSR's opening toolbox:
You have a number of policy problems to solve:

Almost two years have passed since the USA discovered that Secretary
Khrushchev was running a bluff in bragging about Soviet strategic
nuclear superiority. The Americans not only know that the Red Army's
Strategic Rocket Forces have barely a handful of ICBM's capable of
reaching the US. Even then, they are somewhat unreliable and require
very lengthy fueling times to be ready to launch. Meanwhile, the Americans have built up their Minuteman ICBM's which can launch in, well,
a minute, plus a fleet of Polaris nuclear submarines, besides their usual
Strategic Air Command.

The USSR's budget is in miserable shape. While increases in defense spending are possible, they will further strain an economy that is barely delivering an adequate amount of consumer basics. Agriculture in particular
needs major capital investments.

Communism has achieved a signal triumph in Cuba—a homegrown, genu-
inely popular communist insurrection that succeeded. Nothing can be
allowed to snuff out this great victory. But the Americans already have
tried one invasion last year, at the Bay of Pigs. It failed, led by pitiful
reactionary exiles. But the next attempt almost surely will be led by the
American marines.

To solve these problems, you have some hardware (the "software" you
will need to devise or improvise):

The USSR has considerable ground forces at its disposal.
It has Surface-to-Air Missiles (SAMs), ones capable of highly accurate
fire against low-level aircraft, and more expensive (and scarcer) SAMs
capable of bringing down even the high-flying American U-2 spy plane.

It has a good arsenal of battlefield or tactical nuclear warheads, capable of annihilating even a marine invasion force before it ever lands on the beach.

It has no ICBMs to spare, but, given enough time to ship and construct, it can deploy in Cuba Medium Range Ballistic Missiles (MRBMs, which can reach about as far north as Atlanta from Cuba) and Intermediate Range Ballistic Missiles (IRBMs, reach just to Washington, DC).

Using these handouts as rules, and short but clear role sheets, I have gotten students with no simulation experience up and running in under ten minutes. For such a microsimulation with minimal preparation time for the students, the instructor needs to be more hands-on in reminding students what actions are possible. An aggressive Soviet team, for example, needs to be informed that it has extremely limited ways of landing nuclear weapons on the United States's homeland in 1962. An aggressive Cuba must be told that—short of Soviet aid and equipment—it has no way of striking at the United States and will be overrun, even if at great cost to the invaders, if the US decides to overthrow Castro by occupying Cuba. If students are skeptical of the restrictions you impose, you should have some readings and references at the ready for them to consult (after class).

One problem with these simulations, especially if run with few students, is missing roles. Suppose Kennedy wants to talk to Cuban refugees in Florida, but no student has been assigned that role. In these cases, the instructor has to be ready to take it, and any other role needed, temporarily. Bring lots of hats.

Even for these short simulations, perhaps especially so, some postmortem reflections are highly desirable. More times than not, my students have triggered a Soviet-US nuclear exchange. Postmortems lead the students to wonder why—and how—the actual crisis was resolved without incinerating large parts of the planet. Sometimes I pass around the National Security Archive's fascinating volume of collected documents from the crisis.[4] Students are amazed that the same problems and arguments that they just experienced are closely reflected in those materials. Some start to think they could do just as good a job as actual leaders and policy makers, maybe better. Can't have that, can we?

Japan: 1941

Practically all students in this simulation enter it certain they can do better than their historical counterparts. How could any Japanese leader be crazy enough to desire a war with the United States? How could any combination of such leaders actually see their desire prevail as national policy?

Japan: 1941 is a much-honed-down modification of John Moser's excellent Reacting simulation, *Japan, Pan-Asianism, and the West, 1940–41.*[5] Moser's is fairly short itself, but requires more than a single session. *Japan: 1941* can be run in a single afternoon, or even a single hour if the instructor forces the pace.

As with *Missiles*, brief but clear role sheets are indispensable. Here is an example of my condensation of Moser's role sheet for Admiral Oikawa Koshirō:

> In 1930 you received an appointment to the Navy General Staff, and in 1932 you were named commander of the Naval Academy. The following year you were promoted to vice admiral.
>
> You belonged to the Treaty Faction of the navy, viewing the tonnage limits placed on the fleet at the Washington Conference of 1922 and the London Conference of 1930 as perfectly acceptable. Back then, the Treaty Faction was predominant within the admiralty, and had the full support of the civilian government—which preferred a policy of working with the West and promoting international trade. A Fleet Faction, however, saw these treaties as a national humiliation, since Japan had to accept a fleet that was smaller than those of the United States and Great Britain. The Fleet Faction started growing in influence during the early 1930s, while the authority of the civilian government declined. By 1934 the nationalists and militarists were strong enough to issue an announcement that Japan would no longer feel bound by the Washington and London treaties within two years.
>
> Fortunately, the rise of the Fleet Faction did not prevent your career from flourishing, probably because you continued to enjoy the friendship of the emperor. In 1935 you were placed in command of the navy's Third Fleet and in 1938 you were named commander-in-chief of the navy's assets in China. In that capacity you oversaw the bombardment and seizure of many of China's coastal cities in 1938 and 1939. Your efforts were recognized by another promotion—to full admiral—in November 1939.

You left the China Area Fleet in 1940 to take command of the Yoko-suka Naval District, but served in that position for only a few months before learning that Yoshida Zengo had become seriously ill and was stepping down as navy minister. (In fact, this illness was caused by severe pressure from the army and Matsuoka to accept an alliance with Germany, an alliance Yoshida had strongly opposed.) By virtue of seniority you have been tapped as his successor. You now find yourself in Tokyo as the navy's official representative on the cabinet: the navy minister. You too believe the German alliance was a mistake, but it's a done deal.

Your Objectives:

Avoid a Northward Advance at all costs!
The United States has been building up its navy tremendously in recent years; Japan's needs to keep pace. A war with the Soviets will see the army hog resources and funds the navy badly needs.
Get the cabinet to endorse the occupation of southern Indochina—a limited Southward Advance.
War against Britain and America is very risky, but the navy needs southern Indochinese bases to prepare for it if it comes. The Vichy French regime in Saigon can easily be bullied into allowing Japanese forces to enter the colony, so it can be carried out with little cost.
Remain navy minister at the end of the game.
The upper ranks of the navy are filled with ambitious admirals who are looking for powerful positions in the government. Some who remember your support for the Washington and London naval treaties may seek to discredit you in an effort to secure your job for themselves. Also, you could lose your job if the navy chief of staff, Nagano, orders you to resign. If he does so you must obey, so your best bet is to convince him not to give you such an order. Compromise with his views as necessary.

In about a single page, this role sheet manages to give student-Oikawa a good sense of where the admiral stands within the Imperial Navy and the Japanese government. It makes clear what actual policies he wants and his crucial relationship with Admiral Nagano. Let's take a look at his counterpart in the Imperial Army, Tōjō Hideki:

The Japanese Army in the 1920s offered little opportunity for promotion, but you bucked the odds and by the end of the decade had risen to the rank of colonel and were entrusted with the post of bureau chief. Your reputation for sharpness of mind and the ability to make quick decisions competently led your colleagues to give you the nickname *kamisori* (razor). In the 1930s, when money began flowing again to the armed forces, you rose quickly. In 1934 you were promoted to major general and appointed chief of the Army Ministry's Personnel Department. Later that same year you received a brigade command and, soon after, were named commander of the unit of the Kempeitai (the military's secret police) attached to the Kwantung Army in Manchukuo.

In Manchukuo, you became associated with a group of bureaucrats attached to the regime and to state-sponsored businesses such as the South Manchuria Railway Company. (Several of these men—Matsuoka Yōsuke, Hoshino Naoki, Kishi Nobusuke, and Kaya Okinori—are represented in the game). Together you concluded many deals for the development of Manchuria, but also for the lining of your own pockets. In particular, you made an agreement by which you allowed Japan's criminal underworld—the infamous yakuza—to sell opium in occupied China, in return for a massive share of the take.

In early 1938, after the "China Incident" had begun, you were recalled to Japan to serve as vice-minister of war. Soon afterward you were given the post of inspector-general of army aviation, a position you held for two years until the new prime minister, Konoe Fumimaro, chose you for the post of war minister. As a result, you are now the most powerful soldier in Japanese politics (although you remain subordinate to the army chief of staff, your old friend Sugiyama), at a critical time in your country's history.

Objectives:

Remain army minister.

Be sure to represent the army's position to the cabinet faithfully. Otherwise you will be fired.

Under no condition is Japan to abandon Wang Jingwei's regime in China, or withdraw from any part of China.

Jiang Jieshi is on the ropes. He should not be left off them. Under no circumstances should any of our gains in China be sacrificed or compromised.

At the very least, begin preparations for the Northward Advance.

Here is a chance to finish off the hated Soviets, as Germany is about to attack them in Europe. We should seize it!

Become prime minister, if possible, while remaining as war minister.

Konoe's Imperial Rule Assistance Association is a great idea, but Konoe is not the man to lead it. He questions himself much too often and lacks the steel backbone of a military man—like you.

IMPORTANT: As army minister, you represent the army in the cabinet. Be sure that your vote there conforms to the army's wishes. Army Chief of Staff Sugiyama can remove you from your position at will (and send you to the Chinese Front, shudder!!).

Tōjō's succinct role sheet is likewise clear on his position and objectives. And anyone running *Japan: 1941* will see immediately that on certain issues (Southward vs. Northward Advance) the navy and army are going to clash.

This clash is dramatically sharpened by the main teaching point of this simulation, one that is drilled into the students by earlier course lectures (if it is part of a course) or a brief introductory talk by the instructor (if it is a stand-alone exercise): Imperial Japan has no way of reconciling differences between the army and navy. Both are coequal in determining Japan's foreign and defense policies. Invariably, impasse results. The students begin to see the difficulties of Japan's strategic position in 1941, and the even greater difficulties in attempting to address them rationally.[6]

The Guns of August

During the Missile Crisis, President Kennedy—an avid reader of history, not just a maker of it—often thought of a book he and thousands of others in the United States had just finished: *The Guns of August*, by Barbara Tuchman. Tuchman's study traced the origins of the First World War during the summer of 1914. It emphasizes how inflexible doctrine, thinking, and protocols locked in the major European powers, turning a local crisis between Austria-Hungary and Serbia into a general European war that would destroy a generation and, by its end, nearly all the governments which entered it. Kennedy used the lessons to avoid similarly blind decisions in 1962. But the fatal events of 1914 themselves can make for a riveting classroom simulation that can be run in an afternoon or two.

As in any very brief simulation, thorough preparation by the instructor is imperative. Role sheets are the heart of that preparation. Do you want composite characters, such as generic senior army officers of Germany, France, and Russia? These are easier for you to write, but lack the draw-in power of real characters. Do you want to include roles for Serbia, the other Balkan states, even the United States? The choices you make will affect the dynamics of the simulation.[7] They should be made with such effects in mind, not simply assumptions that one country or another simply must be represented by a student-character. Especially for these sorts of simulations, you as instructor can wear hats—take on roles temporarily— as necessary.

Never forget rules, either. Students want to know what they can, and cannot, do. When I have run *Guns*, I have kept things very simple, since it does not have two or three teams, but five or more. Each nation can negotiate all it wishes with anyone it wishes. But it can only take two actions. It can mobilize its army. And it can declare war on and invade other nations. Tuchman-like, these are inflexible; once begun they cannot be taken back. Nor can they be hidden from anyone else. Moreover, mobilization must precede declaration and invasion. Whichever nation begins mobilization first gains a major military advantage over late starters.

These are simple rules. They are easy to grasp quickly. But they impart a great deal of tension into the afternoon's simulation. Germany and Russia might be on the brink of a negotiated solution, but each fears the other will spring a surprise mobilization, or that neither can control an impulsive Austria which, if it mobilizes, will have invasion-ready troops along Russia's border, not just Serbia's. The pace of negotiations among the various national teams often becomes frenetic. Proof is the sprained ankle of one diplomat in one of my sessions, injured in a mad race between capitals while negotiating stairs.[8] While it is possible that war is averted, students gain a new appreciation for how easily Europe slipped over the precipice that summer.

Unlimited Possibilities

If one or more of the published simulations, like *Greenwich Village*, *Stages*, *Galileo*, or any of the dozens available at the Reacting to the Past project site, fits your classroom needs, by all means use them. That is why their authors made them available, after all. But if they do not quite fit— perhaps they require too few or too many students, perhaps their subject does not fully integrate with your instructional objectives, perhaps you are reluctant to commit as many of your class sessions to them as they desire—I want this chapter to encourage you to try your hand at designing your own, custom-made for your own class.[9] I realize this sounds like a challenge. That's how it sounded to a group of graduate students in my recent teaching practicum, where I required them to devise their own simulations, and gave them one week to do it. Here is what they came up with:

Pizarro and the Fall of the Incan Empire

Giovanni proposed this classic first contact situation ideal for a simulation of very short to intermediate length. It has vivid roles: Atahualpa and Pizarro lead among them, but with great possibilities for de Soto, Cinquinchara and, if more sessions are possible, religious figures and potential allies of either side from Incan and other Native American leaders. Historically, the result was the Battle of Cajamarca in 1532 and the resulting Spanish conquest. But other possibilities are plausible, and perhaps even probable, especially if Atahualpa's brother Huáscar is put into play. It is certainly possible to give a riveting lecture on the battle and conquest. Many readings are available. But the high drama of this historical confrontation can make for even higher levels of student engagement in what many might have thought was just a distant and dusty past.

Cholera in New York City

The Reacting site already has an excellent cholera simulation of its own, set in London in 1854.[10] Lorna's takes place in New York twenty-two years earlier and is less a conflict over water supplies than a drama of personal decisions and search for information. As such, it directly confronts a dilemma facing any historical simulation: how to present the unknown or, to put it negatively, how to disguise what has become known. In this case, we know today how cholera is spread, what public health measures can be taken to limit that spread, and what individual steps we can take to limit our exposure. But in 1832 none of these was known. How then to reproduce that uncertainty? One set of Lorna's roles include doctors and city leaders, who must decide if quarantine measures or port closures are necessary. A merchant family has the means to leave the stricken city, but doing so will badly damage their business. A poor family has no means to leave, but must choose whether to board themselves in, do without for a while, and hope for the best, or continue working outside, providing for themselves hand-to-mouth and hope they are among the lucky survivors.

Public health simulations face the unknowability paradox most directly, but it is present in many others. Atahualpa and the Incans had never seen white men before and had to determine whether they were men or gods. They had no idea what a horse was, only that the Spanish somehow knew how to ride one. Is it possible to introduce these unknowns into a simulation?

It is, but the historian's inclination to fill in the fullest context possible must be trimmed a bit. Naming the malady "cholera" is a dead giveaway and invitation for any student to consult a search engine. But what if the simulation called it "descolada" instead?[11] Now the mystery is restored. The disease could be anything, spread any way, with unknown malignancy and effects.

Pizarro's horses might become Sevai[12] or even just Dragons. Maybe they breathe fire? Have indestructible hides? Supernatural intelligence? None of these attributes may be historically accurate, not even close, but we are not after literal accuracy here. We are trying to recreate the uncertainty, even misgiving and fear, that the Incans must have felt in confronting the unknown. Simulations can do this better than the best lecturers.

Midway, 1942

The theme of Will's simulation is also the unknown, though in this case there is no need for fiction of any kind. It is set in the spring of 1942. Japan has just completed a series of stunning victories over the British and the United States from Pearl Harbor to Singapore. Japanese plans had called for a consolidation of gains and establishment of a defensive perimeter that the Western powers would find discouragingly costly to attack, but the speed and magnitude of triumphs now led Tokyo to a temptation to continue offensive operations to break the West's will and ability to continue the fight at all. The question was where and with what new objectives?

Will characterized his simulation as a sort of the old classic board game Battleship, where each player in turn blindly guesses where the other has placed his ships, only receiving a reply of "hit" or "miss" for each shot taken. It is a good comparison. Japan can commit all, some, or none of its Combined Fleet assets to one of three avenues: a continuation of its

Southward Advance into Australia, likely forcing Churchill from power if it succeeds; a return to Hawaiian waters to flush out and destroy the US aircraft carriers that were missed at Pearl Harbor; or a raid into the Indian Ocean, possibly to occupy the island of Ceylon and cripple Britain's hold over India. All three represented serious threats to the United States and Britain, which had joint resources unequal to the Japanese. Historically, superior intelligence capabilities and some luck allowed the United States to parry Japan's efforts against Australia (at the Battle of the Coral Sea) and then off the Hawaiian islands (at Midway). But history could have turned out far differently. Uncertainties—unknowables—abound. Roles could include US, British, and Japanese leaders, but if numbers allow it would be fascinating to add Indians and Australians as well.

The Sepoy Mutiny

Jocelyn proposed a simulation centered on the Sepoy Mutiny against the British East India Company in 1857. It was far from a binary affair, however, and her simulation offered a rich variety of possible roles. The Sepoys attempted a restoration of Mughal rule over much of India, but other Indians refused to join their rebellion or, as with the Sikhs, actively fought against it. Some embraced the social and cultural mores of the British; others were appalled by the new, Western ways. Political and religious differences had their impact. Nor were factional divisions confined to the Indian side of things. Some British joined the Sepoys. Others began to argue that many of the troubles in India were due to the exercise of sovereignty there by the Company instead of the British Crown. While unsympathetic to the Sepoys and their methods, they proposed (and historically would achieve) fundamental revisions in the way India was ruled, revisions that included the abolition of the Company. While the richness of the possible roles represents the central appeal of this simulation, it too has plenty of room for the role of (mis)information: the British press was abuzz for months with lurid stories of varying accuracy that played a fundamental role in the mutiny's outcome.

The Other 9/11

Most in the US associate September 11 with the terrorist attacks on New York and Washington. Matias' simulation reminds us that there was another bloody 9/11, in 1973 when Chilean president Salvador Allende died and his government was overthrown by a military coup led by General Augusto Pinochet. Besides these two protagonists, other roles exist for their Chilean supporters, from truck drivers (whose strike sparked the crisis), to housewives, to dedicated socialists. Outsiders could be cast as well: Richard Nixon, Henry Kissinger, and Fidel Castro all were involved, as were several large US multinational corporations. The simulation could work well as a very brief exercise focused on the week of the coup, or it could allow for more options by beginning much earlier. What if Allende had agreed to Cuban arms for a popular militia that might have resisted Pinochet's army, for example? A postmortem of this simulation would allow students to look at the complicated motivations behind the coup, and its historical success, more deeply than most lectures or discussions.

The Potsdam Summit

Another ideal candidate for a brief but illuminating simulation would be Ken's idea for one centered around the great power summit at Potsdam in the summer of 1945. The map of Europe must be redrawn, the future of Germany determined. Will Stalin keep to his pledge of bringing the Soviet Union into the war against Japan? Will Truman divulge the actual nature and existence of the US atomic bombs? Will the Japanese emperor be spared as an institution or in his person in any surrender offer to Tokyo? What of the future of Britain and its empire as Clement Attlee takes the prime ministership from Winston Churchill in midconference? The fate of the world hangs in the balance, brought back to life in just two or three class sessions.

Ocean Hill-Brownsville, 1968

Perhaps not the fate of the world, but the future of public education and relations between key groups in the largest US city were at stake in Gabe's simulation of the Ocean Hill-Brownsville teachers' strike that further roiled the United States in the pivotal year of 1968. The first day of school that fall saw three citywide strikes of monumental importance. The relatively new but powerful United Federation of Teachers (UFT) began a walkout over the dismissal of its members from an experimental school district in the city's Ocean Hill-Brownsville neighborhood. The fired teachers were mainly Jewish; the district mostly Black and Puerto Rican. Neighborhood leaders had demanded schools with local control and staffed, they hoped, with teachers of color. The result was a deep fracture of what might have been natural allies over civil rights and workplace issues. Instead, similar disagreements arose elsewhere in the city, a full-blooded row over local versus central control of city schools, and sharp group cleavages that would affect the city's mayoral elections for decades thereafter.

This simulation could be a short one focused on the immediate issues of how to end the strike and on what (or whose) terms. Or it could be extended through several class sessions and simulated years, including neighborhood advocates from across the city, other unions, and a wide array of political hopefuls and leaders, and even some UFT holdouts from the older Teachers Union who would set up their own "freedom schools" during the strike. Representatives from Manhattan's wealthy elite, from Mayor John Lindsay to *The New York Times*, usually supported Ocean Hill-Brownsville community leaders. The outer boroughs turned strongly against them in an early display of what would later be called the populism of the right.

King, X, Connor, and the Kennedys

Danielle's proposed simulation also takes place in the turbulent 1960s, encompassing a wide variety of characters involved in the US civil rights movement of that decade. In an ambitious effort, she proposes to examine what a simulation does best: the "what ifs" of that movement. What if major organizations such as the Student Nonviolent Coordinating Council and Southern Christian Leadership Conference had cooperated better and longer than they historically did? What if they parted ways earlier, and drifted even further apart? What if Martin Luther King Jr. had made different choices at different points? What if those choices had avoided his assassination in 1968? What if the Nation of Islam and Malcolm X had followed different paths? What if Theophilus Eugene "Bull" Connor, long-standing chief of public safety in Birmingham, Alabama, had played a cooler hand? What if President Jack Kennedy had decided to put real civil rights legislation at the top of his priorities at the start of his presidency instead of focusing on Cold War concerns? Or what if those concerns drove him toward such legislation earlier than they did? What if his brother, Attorney General Robert Kennedy, had elected to deploy federal coercion more powerfully, from the FBI to the federal marshals, than he came to (at least in the latter case)?

This simulation has the potential for dozens of independent roles and exceptionally engaging characters, King, X, Connor, the Kennedys, even J. Edgar Hoover. It also presents exceptionally rich opportunities to see the events and choices of these years from perspectives many students never considered. While it would require extensive preparation in its most expansive form, that preparation is likely to achieve impressive results in the classroom.

Cortés in Mexico

Although Fernando and Giovanni did not consult about their simulations in advance, their proposals would make a wonderful twin-simulation exercise and a natural pairing. Hernán Cortés may have wanted riches when his expedition left Cuba in 1519, but he achieved far more, some of it to the consternation of his fellow Spaniards. But the Aztecs were hardly unified themselves. The Texcocans had been among the Aztecs' most powerful allies, but were turned, in part through the linguistic and diplomatic talents of an indigenous slave known as Doña Marina. Aztec leader Moctezuma ended up done in by his own people, or was he? Cortés made a fateful error in entrusting the security of Aztec nobles to Pedro de Alvarado, or did he? Let the debates begin in Fernando's simulation with outstanding possibilities for students in its postmortem session.

Trying Matters

Trials are surefire successes as classroom exercises. One of this book's core examples has been *The Trial of Galileo*. Even without being familiar with it, three students in my practicum either proposed or, in one case, actually ran a simulated trial.

Dafina proposed a trial of Napoleon Bonaparte's place in history. Did he forward the ideals of the Enlightenment or betray them? Was he France's savior or tyrant? Was he adored by the leading lights of his age or despised by them? Participants, whether to give testimony, sit in judgment, or both, would include church leaders, heads of state, their domestic opponents, the spirit of Louis XVI, and the impressions of Lord Byron and Francisco Goya.

Bonnie suggested a trial of an actual person, with its outcome to affect the simulation's events to follow. England's Charles I was tried in the House of Commons and, historically, executed in January 1649. One actual effect of that trial was another one: of the signers of Charles' death warrant. They would be tried and put to death, through spectacular and excruciating means, eleven years later. Stakes would be high for many of the student-roles in this one. Those roles would include the straightforward choices of Charles' loyalists (and royalists), Cromwell's Puritans, members of Parliament opposed to Charles but unfond of Cromwell, Scottish Presbyterians with their own religious quarrels with all comers, and as many named aristocratic and secular notables as class size allows.

Jocelyn, who had already proposed a simulation on the Sepoy Mutiny, actually ran a simulation in her recitation section on the trial of Socrates (399 BCE) on the charges of impiety against the gods and corruption of Athenian youth. A few day's preparation of roles and role sheets led to an animated session that had her students beg to do others for the rest of the semester. The box of Pandora had been opened.

As these examples should illustrate, it is not difficult to imagine simulations of immediate and direct use in your courses. As with any instruction, simulations do require preparation beforehand and, perhaps, a willingness to let students take the reins that some of us might find initially uncomfortable. But the payoffs are immense, in student learning and student interest. Perhaps even better, you as instructor will learn more from your students than might ever have been possible through more traditional means. Simulations animate classrooms because they engage students. They work. Try some. You and your students will like them.

9

Can You Beat Churchill?

My editor suggested the above title for this book. It catches the eye. And, we thought, helps describe why students are attracted to simulations in the classroom. It is certainly true that, in my simulation *Rivalries*, the student representing Churchill faces truly daunting challenges.

Can Your *Students* Beat Churchill?

At the start of *Rivalries'* real world in 1936, Churchill had enjoyed a bit of luck. He had remained outside government through the Ethiopian crisis, during which Britain's official position had been ambivalent and ultimately embarrassing. Churchill had wanted a cabinet post and had refrained from public criticism of British attempts to buy off Italian aggression through offering Mussolini what amounted to a bloodless victory. As things turned out, Churchill benefited from not being a party to what amounted to, and what he himself would later call, appeasement.

The actual Churchill's experience highlights the first and most fundamental obstacle for any student-Churchill. Just like history's Stanley Baldwin and Neville Chamberlain, all the other students on the British team
know that Churchill is hungry for power. They also know that he means
to use fear of a rising German menace as a path to power. And they know
that, in the world of the simulation, that menace might be real or it might
not. And, even if it were real, a confrontation with Germany likely would
produce two unwanted results. As a leading British diplomat put it at the
time, a bitter struggle against Germany might be won, but then, "It would
only mean communism in Germany and France."[1] And such a struggle
would also propel Churchill into the prime ministership, not an outcome
most British Conservatives relished.

Churchill is somewhat odious to the other members of the British team
because many of his positions seemed almost reactionary. He stubbornly
fought against the grant of dominion status within the British Empire to
India, managing to anger even most members of the Conservative Party.
And just as he was finding support for his strident stance against Hitler and for rearmament among some British labor and socialist leaders,
Churchill embarked upon a fierce and fiercely unpopular defense of soon-
to-be-crowned King Edward VIII, who had scandalized press and public
by declaring his intention to marry a woman from the US as soon as her
divorce (from her second husband, no less) became final. By late 1936,
Churchill thought his career in politics was finished.

Rivalries does not put the obstacles of defense of empire and king directly in the path of a student-Churchill, but it comes close. There is a German Policy Option, "Turn King Edward," that badly hampers Britain's
ability to attempt Policy Options of its own until a British option forcing
Edward's abdication succeeds.[2] Student-Churchill, like the historical one,
will have to decide whether to support the king and risk political backlash
or stand aside and betray a key feature of her or his character. A British Policy Option, if it succeeds, grants independence—not just dominion
status—to India. There will be considerable pressure from the British
Labour Party—and the United States—to attempt this grant. Student-
Churchill will have a hard time resisting it.

Especially if she or he never becomes prime minister in the first place.
The real Churchill's ascent to that office, in the fraught days of May 1940,
had begun only with Hitler's move against the rump of Czechoslovakia

in total violation of the Munich Agreement of September 1938 which Chamberlain had boasted, had achieved, "peace for our time." Churchill's long years of warning about the Nazi menace revived his credibility and his chances for a return to a cabinet position.

Even then, it was hardly a sure thing. Churchill's cries in early 1939 for a fresh approach to the Soviet Union were met with incredulity by most British leaders, especially among the Conservatives. They doubted, with good reason, that the Soviets had either the capacity or the will to resist Germany, doubts solidified by the Nazi-Soviet nonaggression pact of August. They believed that Soviet communism represented a death-challenge to Western civilization that would last for generations, German Nazism a passing fever that would vanish as soon as most Germans forgot their infatuation with Hitler's rash promises and risky policies.

Fortunately for history's Churchill, that infatuation allowed Hitler to menace Poland by summer's end, and even Chamberlain had agreed, in the aftermath of Czechoslovakia's end, to a guarantee of Poland's borders. But Chamberlain remained convinced that, just as Hitler had shied from war over Czechoslovakia, he would prefer a peaceful adjustment of claims over Poland. Even after Germany invaded Poland on September 1, Chamberlain clung to hopes for a swift, largely diplomatic resolution. The invasion, however, compelled him to bring Churchill into the cabinet, on the sensible grounds that it was better to have Winston inside the tent urinating out than outside irrigating in. Given the historical Churchill's often soaring speechmaking skills, it is hard to fault Chamberlain.

After Chamberlain delayed a formal declaration of war against Germany and continued discussions with the Nazis while their troops rampaged through Poland, British hard-liners urged Churchill to lead a parliamentary revolt against the prime minister. Churchill demurred, refusing to divide Britain as it (he hoped and believed) was about to finally go to war. He not only entered Chamberlain's war cabinet, but was also made Admiralty First Lord, a post he had occupied during the First World War.[3]

That earlier tenure had ended in disgrace and political ruin. Then Churchill had masterminded British amphibious landings in the Dardanelles, to knock the Ottoman Empire out of that war and restore a reliable pipeline of aid to Tsarist Russia. The landings had failed badly, and while Churchill had insisted that the strategy was sound but its execution bungled by subordinates, he had taken the fall.

Undeterred by the results of his earlier gamble, in 1939 Churchill proposed another: a British naval offensive to seize control of the Baltic Sea and deprive Germany of crucial imports of iron ore and other strategic resources from Scandinavia. It was wildly risky, particularly in the face of German airpower, which Churchill badly underestimated. It was never attempted and, better yet for Churchill, never revealed to the British public during the war.

Churchill was not one to give up easily. After shelving the proposed expedition into the Baltic, he proposed obtaining the same objective by landing British troops in Scandinavia with a special effort to seize Swedish iron ore mines. Reaching those mines was nearly as risky as the proposed expedition, but Churchill believed Mother Nature could ease his task. The ore could be shipped from Sweden directly to Germany in the warmer months, but in winter Swedish ports froze over, compelling the ore to go to Narvik, Norway, and thence to German destinations. Getting at Narvik was well within Churchill's reach, either by sowing mines in the waters right off that port or actually landing British forces to take the port itself.

But Hitler also realized Narvik's vulnerability and determined to occupy it himself, along with all of Norway and Denmark for good measure. He beat Churchill to the punch. Churchill initially thought the German occupation an advantage for Britain, exposing Norway's long shoreline, and its precious off-coast water route for the iron ore, now open to British naval attack. He failed to appreciate how German control of the coast also conferred control of airfields along it. German warplanes would make British ships easy targets. Churchill's efforts to seize Narvik were repulsed repeatedly.[4] By the start of May 1940, it was clear that Norway had been lost—a huge setback.

The setbacks were just beginning. The British public, expecting easy pickings in Norway, was shocked by Churchill's admission of defeat. Days later, Germany invaded Holland, Belgium, and France. But if it had been Churchill who had informed Parliament of the loss, it turned out to be Chamberlain who absorbed the blame. His boast, before the race for Norway had begun, that Hitler had "missed the bus," now came back to haunt him and threaten his grip on the prime ministership. Verbal attacks in Parliament on Chamberlain's leadership grew brutal. When the opposition Labour Party moved a vote of no-confidence, Chamberlain indignantly replied that his Conservative Party members would sustain his leadership. Most did, but one hundred of them did not, a real shock to the prime minister, who concluded that he had no choice but to form a new cabinet with representation from both Labour and the bolting Conservatives. When Labour made clear that it would not join any cabinet with Chamberlain at its head, the path to the prime minister was at last open to Churchill.

The popular tale now turns to Churchill Triumphant, the man who embodied the English spirit, the fighting bulldog, who saw Britain through the dark days of fighting alone against Hitler, who helped forge an enduring alliance with the United States and an improbable one with the Soviet Union, able to see a Great Britain as one of the big three powers sitting at summit conferences at Cairo, Yalta, and Potsdam that would forge a new world order by the close of the Second World War.

There is nothing incorrect in this tale, but it passes over a number of considerations if any student is really out to beat Churchill. Churchill carefully cultivated a personal relationship with US President Franklin Roosevelt. Yet Roosevelt pressed hard and often successfully for wartime agreements[5] undermining the British Empire and Commonwealth, from new universal trade arrangements to independence for India. Churchill would see Germany's defeat, but Britain hardly emerged unchanged or unscathed. British forces would defend the Suez canal, only to see it lost to Egyptian nationalism a decade later. Singapore, the British bastion in the Pacific, would fall to Japan in the largest single military defeat in Britain's history, and the British Empire in the Pacific would, to all effects, cease to exist after Japan's surrender.

Any student-Churchill in *Great Power Rivalries* who wants to beat Churchill's historical performance will need skill, luck, and perhaps even heroics. Churchill's admission back into government was beyond his power; it required confirmation that Germany really was the top menace to Britain. His assumption of the admiralty portfolio was in no small part due to his pledge of loyalty to Chamberlain and Chamberlain's grace and recognition of Churchill's political utility. His rise to the prime ministership required British failure abroad and an improbable and badly handled party insurrection at home. His victory over Germany established his legend and ensured a statue outside Westminster and would have to be equaled. His failure to ensure the maintenance of British empire and power over the long term would have to be surpassed. Can you beat Churchill? If you are a student in a class that uses historical simulations, like *Rivalries*, you are very welcome to try. Experience history through Churchill's eyes. See if you can do better than he did. Your path will not be easy. You will not be the giant portrayed in Churchill's own account, prophetically warning the cowards around you that Hitler meant business, and rising miraculously to leadership, then victory. You will have to learn how to navigate the reefs and shoals of British politics, and do so with an eye to developments in Europe and the world that will require responses with a perfect mixture of prudence and risk. But, most of all, you will have to learn.

How Churchill Beat Churchill

Winston Churchill was not just Great Britain's most famous prime minister. He was also a prolific writer of histories, including his own. His most famous work starred himself, a six-volume collection appropriately titled *The Second World War.*[6] In it, Churchill offered an interpretation that has become the dominant narrative of the war, especially its origins, so dominant that it has been a central influence on US foreign policy ever since.[7] Not coincidentally, Churchill's magisterial work also cemented his place in history as that most famous prime minister. Churchill the historian was better than Churchill the actual leader.

In essence, Churchill argued that the Western democracies fundamentally misunderstood Adolf Hitler's rise, determination, fanaticism, and aggressive goals during most of the 1930s. Churchill's chief villain, or at least fool and knave, was Neville Chamberlain, prime minister from 1937 to 1940. Chamberlain's policy of "appeasement," a term that ever since has been used as a high insult to anyone's policies, was the epitome of this misunderstanding. It led to Britain allowing Hitler to have the Rhineland, then Austria, then parts of Czechoslovakia, then all of it, until Chamberlain belatedly and still tepidly woke up to the threat of Nazism and, in a parting gesture of futility, warned Hitler not to commit aggression against Poland. When Hitler did anyway, Chamberlain went to war—too late to prevent what became a global catastrophe. In Churchill's volumes, Chamberlain is doubly damned because he had early and persistent warnings about the evils of Nazism—from Churchill himself. Chamberlain waited too long because he was too trusting of and naïve about Hitler's true nature, and he was too eager to avoid possibly wasteful spending on Britain's military and defense. The lesson could not be clearer: the first signs of a nation's "aggression" toward its neighbors must be nipped in the bud, by threat or use of armed force if necessary. Appeasing aggressors only encourages them to demand more. Churchill was right; Chamberlain wrong.

These are facts. This is historical knowledge. Woe to anyone who questions them. People, especially students, don't like questions. They want answers, just so long as those answers are right (as, on the test) and easy to remember.[8] For years, I tried to introduce doubt in my lecture course on the Second World War. Chamberlain was aware of the Nazi danger. He advocated rearmament as early as 1935. Was it not possible to see appeasement as a relatively risk-free way—for Britain, at least—to attempt to avoid a war that Chamberlain rightly saw would be a disastrous tragedy, or at least delay such a war until Britain was more fully prepared? Most of my students would have none of it. My essay assignment on the origins of the war invariably saw a comfortable majority confidently blaming Chamberlain's cowardice. In any contest against Churchill, I was badly outmatched.

Except one. Most students on the British teams in *Rivalries* saw things in much more complex terms, much more realistic ones. And not just the student-Chamberlain, naturally defensive about her character. Most members of the British team questioned history's Churchill's case in a way few students in my lecture class did. Going to war with Germany might turn out badly, they realized. We have a global empire to safeguard and limited resources, they understood. When my lecture class held discussions on the origins of the war in Europe, Chamberlain actually had some defenders who said: it's much more complicated than who was right or wrong in retrospect.

What was going on? Nothing particularly new: the difference between teaching and learning has been recognized for decades, if not more than a century. An example of this recognition would be a passionate and provocative piece published in 1995 appropriately entitled "From Teaching to Learning—a New Paradigm for Undergraduate Education," by Robert Barr and John Tagg.[9] They argue that the current model of education confuses teaching with learning. A teacher imparts information. The students passively receive it and regurgitate it on an examination. They leave the exam, promptly forgetting the information, none the more educated, or wiser, for having received it. Even more critically, Barr and Tagg assert, most educational institutions don't even bother evaluating what their graduates have actually learned—what they can do that they couldn't before entry. These institutions are content to count up the credits and hand out their diplomas and degrees. It is like handing out boards and bricks to prospective carpenters and masons and telling them to figure out how to build a house.

Barr and Tagg would prefer to tear down the ossified structures of education. Learning outcomes, not packaged courses-for-credits, would define these new institutions. Among these outcomes would be writing, problem solving, and effective team participation. How are these outcomes to be achieved?

> If the model in the Instruction Paradigm is that of delivering a lecture, then the model in the Learning Paradigm is that of designing and then playing a team game. A coach not only instructs football players, for example, but also designs football practices and the game plan; he participates in the game itself by sending in plays and making other decisions. The new faculty role goes a step further, however, in that faculty not only design game plans but also create new and better "games," ones that generate more and better learning.[10]

Barr and Tagg conclude with the admission that changing paradigms will be hard. Do away with set-credit courses? Abandon graduation requirements fixed by credit hours? They offer no clear way to shift from teaching to learning, but reassure their readers that change is possible, citing three examples. Swiss watchmakers were horrified by the idea of a quartz watch but eventually embraced it. Audiences jeered Stravinsky's *The Rite of Spring*; now they revere it. And the church has admitted that Galileo was right.

True enough, but not exactly encouraging. The church revised its 1633 condemnation of Galileo only in 1992. It took eighty years from the discovery of quartz's potential timekeeping properties to the production of the first watch. The choreography for 1913's *Rite* would not be attempted again for decades.

This is fairly depressing stuff and it only gets worse. Barr and Tagg are hardly alone in criticizing the main delivery, teaching-not-learning-centered method of education. The literature on these issues is vast. It is also inconclusive, diffuse, sometimes polemical, often unhelpful.

The polemics tend to take two tacks. On the one hand, traditional teaching methods are dismissed as hopelessly outdated, the products of a society needing punctual, disciplined workers for the dawning age of industry. On the other, there is a thrashing condemnation of new learning technology that seems to have rendered students incapable of independent thought and reduced the classroom to an exercise in cut-and-paste, instructors to mere conduits teaching to the test. Neither of these critiques directly addresses the use of simulations, but both deserve summaries of their cases that have implications for that use.

The Industrial Classroom: Failed Model?

Our pattern of learning, from grammar through much of graduate school, is so deeply ingrained that we barely think to consider or question it. We go to our classroom, a bell rings, we start our lessons, which are broken into timed segments by subject. As we progress, we learn to move to a different room with a different teacher as the subject changes. By high school, we might have some leeway in choosing among elective classes. In college we can make up our own schedules from a broad menu of courses, though we have to be sure to meet general education requirements and whatever we need for our chosen major to get a degree upon graduation. A lockstep pattern for a lockstep system. But then what?

Over a century ago, when this system was standardized and instituted, the answer was fairly clear. An industrial society and economy needed workers who had basic reading and arithmetical skills so that they could read machine manuals and see that tools were properly calibrated. Some might rise to professional or managerial posts. These people would need even more literacy, to master the intricacies of law, for example, or numeracy, if they were accountants. A very few might have to learn analytical skills to deduce how best to guide their corporations through the perils of cut-throat capitalism.

Is this model of education obsolete? Are its goals still those we want in the contemporary United States? Studies on these questions fill buildings.

Debates over their answers provoke passion. But I have to address them in some fashion if I am to attempt an assessment of whether historical simulations are effective teaching tools. It is hard to measure effectiveness without some sort of yardstick.

At one end of the spectrum are studies such as Bryan Caplan's *The Case against Education*.[11] Caplan argues that, in many respects, the industrial education system works just fine. Its regimented days and methods emphasize conformity, docility, patience, meticulousness, deference to authority, and a knowledge of what is socially acceptable. Literacy and numeracy remain highly useful skills, and the current education system still teaches these early on.[12] But, according to Caplan, the system also piles on loads of other subjects that impart utterly useless skills. Who needs to learn a foreign language? Certainly not US citizens in a world where everybody uses English. Literature and poetry in the world according to Twitter? The fine arts—as practiced on Instagram?

For Caplan, the measure of effectiveness of learning is how well students are prepared to perform jobs. Except for basic literacy and numeracy in grammar school, vocational and technical programs in high school, and computer science and engineering degrees in college, what students actually learn—if they learn anything—offers nothing directly useful. Sure, the system reinforces conformity, docility, and so on, but having students sit in timed classes in front of a teacher, any teacher, teaching anything, does as much. Teaching to the test stresses such qualities even more. Ironically, at the college level, where standardized testing is absent, professors can lecture on whatever they please, confident that although their students will find nothing marketable in their knowledge of Shakespeare, Kant, Madison, or Friedman, just going through the routine of sitting in class, taking notes, and writing papers and examination demonstrates that they can conform, listen to instruction, and so on. Employers are willing to accept the results—and value degrees—precisely because completion of a degree program, any degree program, so demonstrates. The only real difference between the industrial classroom and the current one is the rise of a self-reinforcing educational establishment that, over time, made acquiring a high school diploma, then a bachelor's degree, and soon something more a fundamental prerequisite to getting a good job or career. Imparting real skills useful in that job or career is done seldom if at all.

If Caplan's analysis is accurate, the outlook is grim for universities, and hardly welcome for most high schools. As purveyors of irrelevant lessons full of useless facts, they should be radically shrunken, their programs abbreviated, and access to them limited to those programs that impart those real skills. What's the point of all those hours students spend as passive lumps listening to lectures on subjects they will never remember, let alone use, as soon as they walk out of the final exam?

Digitized and Online Learning: A New Hope?

The issue of access to—and expense of—degree programs has been a driving force behind the rise of the MOOC: Massive Open Online Course. While certainly not confined to Caplan's categories of real skills, MOOC's have enjoyed their highest (online) enrollments in precisely those areas, from basic mathematics to higher-level computer programming and science. Compared to the traditional brick-and-mortar education, online courses are considerably less expensive and, accessible from home at any hour of the day, more convenient.

Cheap, accessible, and convenient, maybe, but effective? Almost as soon as they were introduced in the early 2010s, MOOCs were criticized on two counts. One actually was accessibility. If a prospective student had no reliable internet connection or a decent computer, the MOOCs might as well have been offered on the moon. The other pointed to the abysmal completion rates. Between 5 and 15 percent of students enrolling in MOOCs actually finish them. The percentage of students completing enough MOOCs to earn a degree is even lower.[13]

There are several reasons for these low completion rates. Without a set classroom and class schedule (and examination time), students just cannot motivate themselves to cross the finish line. Put another way, students cannot motivate themselves to learn. More fundamentally, though, students in MOOCs are lonely.[14] If they get stuck, they cannot raise their hand in class or go to the instructor's office hours. With enrollment often in the thousands, they cannot expect an instant reply to an email from their human teacher.[15] Forming study groups with other students is possible, but quite a bit more challenging than with more traditional courses. For large swaths of subject material, learning in isolation is simply impossible.

Organic chemistry lab at home? Learn how to dribble a soccer- or basket-
ball by watching a video?

As these last examples show, one key to successful and completed learning is to involve the students in groups, with the students in those groups
sharing the objective of achieving a set objective within the course.[16] That is
what a science lab session does, or a team practice—or a simulation.

It turns out that among the set of skills that are directly useful on the
job are the ability to communicate with others and work with them as a
team in accomplishing things. Even Caplan's accountants, statisticians,
engineers, and computer scientists need to master these skills, which cannot be learned in isolation. How can we encourage students to learn these
skills? Are there also other skills we can foster that might have value, even
if they are not as directly connected with job performance?

A paradigm shift in educational institutions is not required to create
learning such skills in them. They all don't have to become like Hampshire
college (itself in a financial bind as these words are being written).[17] You
can show students how to learn for themselves by using simulations in
your regular classes.

Simulations animate classrooms because they engage students. They
engage students because students are human beings. Human beings are
naturally competitive and cooperative. They like to form groups and
play. They demonstrate competitiveness and cooperation by playing—and
inventing—games and their cooperation by forming teams to play those
games. They have done so since they have left records for us to examine. Egyptian relics from 1150 BCE depict people playing Senet and the
Game of Twenty. Some artifacts describe the rules; others are actual game
boards.[18] Go, still avidly played in Japan and elsewhere, originated in
China reputedly around 2300 BCE as *wei-qi*. Accounts of Go matches appear in the Japanese classic *The Tale of Genji*. Plato's *Republic* mentions
the usefulness of *petteia*, a game of capture, in training minds. The Roman
game *latrunculi* (or *latrones*) was a precursor to chess.

Games are ancient. Simulations, especially historical simulations, not
so much. The first widespread academic discussion of simulations dates
from the 1990s. Perhaps not surprisingly, it sprang from the popularity
of computer games in that decade. Quite a few of these had historical
themes, such as *The Oregon Trail*, which put players in the role of families

trying to make their way to the US Pacific Coast,[19] and the classic *Civilization* series, first published in 1991.

At the time, many observers attributed the success of these early simulations to their visual appeal, or "eye-candy." They had maps, usually in color, and images of people, objects, or large terrain features that players could interact with or even alter, such as founding a new city in *Civilization*. While there is no denying that these graphics were more appealing than black-and-white walls of text, the real attraction of these early efforts was their success as dynamic yet playable simulations. It turned out to be quite difficult to get your settler family from Missouri to Oregon. Sometimes a dust storm so delayed progress that a search for water compelled a detour or even death. Bandits or hostility from the local inhabitants could mean a lost cause. Disease or starvation were omnipresent threats.

If anything, simulations like *Civilization* presented even greater challenges. You could found cities and oversee their growth, build armies and navies to protect your civilization's territory. But other civilizations, directed by the game's programming, were doing the same thing, often faster or better than you. Your Greeks might have just finished the Parthenon, your pixel citizens beaming with pride and more productive than ever, when the Roman legions show up in overwhelming strength. Oh well, time to quit game and start over.

Quit-and-start-over was delightfully simple, because all these simulations had only one human player. They were solo exercises. In that sense alone, they were not very good simulations. It may not be possible to negotiate with a dust storm. Locals might be irretrievably hostile. But most human contact, even between civilizations, does not inevitably result in human conflict. One of the chief challenges in the entire series of *Civilization* computer games was trying to have the computer's various civilizations mimic human-led ones by offering alliance, trade, tribute, or neutrality, usually based on the game program's assessment of how strong or rich the two rivals were at first contact.

This mimicry has come a long way since 1991, but it still falls far short of passing the Turing test.[20] Even if the artificial civilizations could be directed by much more sophisticated intelligences, it is not clear that any computer game could accommodate the near-infinite possibilities of interaction that real human-to-human exchanges allow. Limits on machine intelligence and degree of interaction, for now and for some time to come, will prevent even graphically attractive and relatively complex computer games from becoming true simulations in the sense that "You are Winston Churchill. It is January 1936. See if you can do better than he did."

Simulations Are Different: Active and Interactive Learning

The ability of classroom simulations, like *Greenwich Village, The Trial of Galileo, Stages of Power,* or *Great Power Rivalries,* to realize exactly this sort of experience is centered on the stark fact that classrooms offer an ideal way to get real humans to interact with each other as historical figures. The students will learn not only about the figures they represent. They will—and must—learn how to interact with other people, each representing their own figures, in order to advance their goals. They have to compete, but they have to cooperate too. If this sounds a lot like real life—that's a vital lesson the simulation students will learn too. Let's break down just how useful this lesson can be.

Does This Stuff Really Work?

This always struck me as an odd question. The institutions that most rapidly adopted simulations as teaching tools are among the most serious that I know: business, health care, and the military. Harvard Business School professors rave about the effectiveness of simulations in their classes.[21] The school maintains an extensive library of simulations, from how to handle a cyberattack to overcoming cultural differences in managing a multinational corporation. Medical simulations, many mimicking real procedures but in a virtual environment, have become indispensable teaching tools.[22] Military academies similarly use virtual battlefields, but, especially at the war college level, stress competitive grand strategic contests that emphasize communication and team building.

In fact, some of the deepest thinking about simulations as a teaching tool has been done not at Yale, Berkeley, or Chicago, but at the US Marines Command and Staff College in Quantico, Virginia. In 2016, a new professor there, James Lacey, published an insightful article on his experiences discovering the value of simulations over traditional instruction. As he put it,

The students had done the readings, listened to my lecture, stared at the slides, asked a few perfunctory questions, and, most of all, watched the clock. A day or two later, I knew that the overwhelming majority of them barely remembered any of my major points. The best I could hope for was that they at least knew that attacking Syracuse was bad, though I doubted any of them could explain why. In that regard, I find it amusing that at least three war colleges, in the Questions to Ponder they hand to the students, ask a variation of the same question: "Was the attack on Syracuse poor strategy, or good strategy marred by poor execution?" My rejoinder is: "How the #$&#@ would the students know?"

The truth is that if one just reads selected passages from Thucydides' work, it is impossible to comprehend the events and complexities of the multi-decade Peloponnesian War. Moreover, as students rarely have the background or context in which to mentally file the readings, they quickly get lost in a plethora of Greek names, locations, and events. War college professors who believe their graduates know anything about Thucydides besides reciting the mantra "fear, honor, interest" are fooling themselves.[23]

The next year, Lacey had his students simulate elements of the Peloponnesian War, focusing on the Athenian decision to attack Syracuse, a decision almost universally condemned in lectures as key to Athens' eventual defeat. He was amazed at the results:

Remarkably, four of the five Athenian teams actually attacked Syracuse on Sicily's east coast! As they were all aware that such a course had led to an Athenian disaster 2,500 years before, I queried them about their decision. Their replies were the same: Each had noted that the Persians were stirring, which meant there was a growing threat to Athens' supply of wheat from the Black Sea. As there was an abundance of wheat near Syracuse, each Athenian team decided to secure it as a second food source (and simultaneously deny it to Sparta and its allies) in the event the wheat from the Black Sea was lost to them. Along the way, two of the teams secured Pylos so as to raise helot revolts that would damage the Spartan breadbasket. Two of the teams also ended revolts in Corcyra, which secured that island's fleet for Athenian purposes, and had the practical effect of blockading Corinth. So, it turns out there were a number of good strategic reasons for Athens to attack Syracuse. Who knew? Certainly not any War College graduate over the past few decades.[24]

Lacey's experiment clearly had an impact on his colleagues as well as his students. Three of them published a study three years later. In it, they discussed the long tradition in military educational institutions of taking students on "staff rides" to historical battlefield sites. There, they would walk the site, getting a worm's eye view of the geography and scope of the battlefield. Educational, to be sure, but how effective in teaching thinking and leadership skills? The answer was "very" if the exercises instead became "decision game–driven staff rides."[25] That is, if they became historical simulations. Instead of walking along the site, passively taking notes, the students were put into positions—roles—and forced to devise solutions, just like Lacey's student-Athenians.

Just as the professional military is a good example of the value of simulations as learning tools, it is a particularly good counterexample to Caplan's narrow interpretation of useful skills. The military trains soldiers and sailors exactly as Caplan might wish them to: a specific set of skills directly related to their job performance.[26] The problem is that few remain soldiers or sailors forever, and often a veteran's search for employment can be frustrating. One ex-marine complained, "Underwater egress training—when am I ever going to use that?"[27] He was an excellent marksman, and had experience driving heavy vehicles under enemy fire, but these skills were not exactly applicable to the career he was hoping to pursue in civilian life: nursing. Fortunately, the military had the RAND corporation compose a guide for veterans: "Essential Skills Veterans Gain during Professional Military Training."[28] Among the top ones? Oral communication, teamwork and team building, critical thinking, and decision-making. If these sound like skills also taught in classroom simulations, it is because they are.

Why History?

Perhaps simulations do teach skills directly useful to a wide variety of jobs. It's easy to see how a virtual simulation of a heart transplant might save lives, or simulating a cyberattack might save a government or a bank. But is there any value to using simulations to teach history, or are any attempts about as relevant to the real world as teaching that marine underwater egress? Put another way, is there any real usefulness in teaching history in any form?

It turns out that history really shines in teaching key skills like critical thinking. "Critical thinking" is a phrase on everyone's lips. Employers claim to want it. Applicants claim to have it. Countless corporate and academic workshops strive to inculcate it. But what is it? As important, how can we determine whether people are learning it?

Sam Wineburg has given much thought to both these questions. Critical thinking is the ability to make connections and draw conclusions that uncritical thinking would miss. Wineburg presents several useful examples. Each concerned different groups of subjects.

One was a painting of the first Thanksgiving dinner of 1621, done by Jean Leon Gerome Ferris and published in 1932. It depicts an idyllic scene. Befeathered Native Americans are served roasted turkey and trimmings by women in modest Pilgrim dress as menfolk look on, complete with Pilgrim child and dog. Wineburg's study group showed it to thousands of US middle and high school students. Thousands described the scene either as an accurate representation of what actually happened, or as a travesty that obscured the rampant exploitation of Native Americans going on behind the scenes. The key variable in the students' contrasting interpretations was which history textbook they had been reading. Collegiate blogs were not much different, though they tended toward the travesty side of things.[29]

Almost no one noted that Ferris could hardly have been present at that first dinner, and it seems unlikely that he did his painting after researching an array of primary materials documenting the occasion. No one, in other words, looked at the source of the painting itself: Ferris' conception of his subject. Critical thinking tells us more about Ferris' learning, and the world of the 1920s when he painted, than what was or was not going on in 1621.

Trained historians actually tend to do much better at critical thinking than others. A second example: President Benjamin Harrison's proclamation that October 21 would henceforth be a holiday known as Discovery Day (later, Columbus Day). Mostly a collection of anodyne boilerplate, it praises Columbus as "a pioneer of progress and enlightenment" and commends people in the US to celebrate in churches Columbus' devout faith and the guidance that he received from above.

Astute high school students in AP history courses were quick to jump on such phrases. Columbus was out to discover a faster way to the riches of the East, not the glory of God. He was not above exploiting and enslaving the hapless inhabitants of the islands he landed upon, not exactly the pinnacle of progress and enlightenment.

An astute analysis, perhaps, but not critical. When Wineburg asked history doctoral students to look over the proclamation, they swiftly zeroed in on its date—July 1892—not Columbus' actions of five hundred years earlier. Harrison was locked into a tight presidential race against Democrat Grover Cleveland. Every vote counted, and more and more of them were coming from Catholic immigrants, especially from Italy. Harrison's proclamation was an attempt to secure support, and rather cleverly tie people of Italian heritage to US (and hopefully Republican) identity.

Critics might object that Wineburg has rigged the game by pitting high schoolers against doctoral students. His third case offers a more level playing field. The document in hand for this one returns to a Thanksgiving theme, but represents President George Washington's proclamation creating the national holiday in 1789. It is a turgid document, with frequent references to the United States' blessings as made possible by "the great Lord and Ruler of Nations."[30]

Wineburg showed Washington's address to three groups, all highly educated: a group of clergy, one of natural scientists, and a third of historians. The first immediately highlighted Washington's references to the Lord, noting with approval that they showed that Washington was a devout Christian, as all US citizens of his generation surely were. The scientists likewise focused on the religion angle, rather put off that Washington would strongly mix, it seems, affairs of church and state. Wasn't the United States a child of the Enlightenment? What were all these references to God doing in there?

The historians saw something different. They saw the address as a constant and deep plea for national unity and tranquility. Sure, there were religious references, but Washington's thanks were for peaceably establishing "a form of government," "particularly the national One now lately instituted." Acutely aware of the political differences that had led to the new federal constitution, Washington also understood that religious differences, or any other kind, had to be peaceably tolerated within the new union. References to the Lord, yes, but not any to Jesus, Mary, or Abraham.

The critical thinking ability to assess sources is critical itself more than ever in any area of life. The Internet is a swamp of facts, alternative facts, and deliberate, vicious anti-facts. How can you tell what is what?

While historians might be tempted to congratulate themselves,[31] there's a pretty obvious problem not far under the surface. When does that critical thinking light switch on? More fundamentally, what turns that switch on?

If the ability to evaluate sources is the first step in learning critical thinking, we have to figure out how to teach that evaluation. Interestingly, the people who habitually evaluate their sources, besides professional historians, are video gamers. When they attempt to find a strategy guide for the more challenging game content, the first thing they look at is the guide's date. *World of Warcraft, Eve Online* and other multiplayer games have evolved swiftly and substantially over time. Guides even a year old are useless, even counterproductive. Video gamers really do examine sources critically, at least in this respect.

It's great that history professors and doctoral students and lots of video gamers have at least some skill in looking at sources, but how might that skill be taught to others? A bit more negatively, why hasn't it been taught to others, especially students (or majors) in high school or college history courses? That most of these students are not learning it is depressingly clear.[32]

But there is hope. Wineburg noticed that sixth graders became animated in class and involved with historical sources when they looked at the reasons why Rosa Parks refused to yield her bus seat in December 1955. The students delved into Parks' memoirs. They examined exactly where she was sitting on the bus, and how the bus driver acted when she refused to move.[33] They were role-playing, one of the fundamental elements of simulations.

Simulations work at even younger ages. John Hunter has been using his own simulation, *World Peace,* in his classrooms since 1978. Fourth-grade classrooms. His *World Peace* is not a *Candyland* or *Chutes and Ladders.* He has six national or quasi-national teams, often set in conflict, plus no fewer than fifty crises confronting his students, from pandemics to climate change. It is contemporary, not historical, but it stresses exactly those group and communication skills students of any age should master.[34]

The connection between the active learning required in any simulation and the acquisition of critical assessment of sources and considering solutions to problems appears in the oddest places.[35] Mark Bauerlein has written a scathing critique of the lack of critical thinking, and presence of virtual illiteracy, in his book, *The Dumbest Generation.* He observes that young people don't read much beyond tweet-length material and are incredulous when an instructor asks for more—"You mean the *whole book?*"[36] They can google just fine and cut-and-paste with the best of them. But actual analysis? Still, even in his criticisms, Bauerlein observed that young people who played *Age of Empires II* learned more about the Crusades than from any of their history classes, and the various iterations of Sid Meier's classic *Civilization* did a pretty good job in getting young minds to think about connections between technology and economics.[37]

Why do even such cynics as Bauerlein concede that people actually learn from games? Why do people who otherwise surf the internet uncritically take care to assess strategy guides as sources? Because they understand that their choices make a difference, and those choices must be based on a sound foundation of what the game looks like and their place in it. The fundamental dynamic of simulations drives students toward assessment of the sources they must base their decisions upon.

Still, doubters remain. In February 2020, the *American Historical Review*[38] published a set of reviews of Reacting simulations. Among the more critical was David Pace's piece. Pace argued that the simulations appeared more directed toward conveying to students—albeit in different fashion—historians' views of what happened in those simulations' subject material rather than teaching those students how to learn how those views were formulated. He also doubted that even most college students had the "positional reasoning required by such simulations."

These are serious charges. The first maintains that the instructional objective of simulations is no different from more traditional teaching (instead of learning) methods. The students are spoon-fed documents. They take these at face value. They assume roles that try to use these documents to forward their position.[39] They might be more actively involved in class rather than being passive notetakers, but is there a different sort of actual learning going on?

This criticism glides over one of the fundamental facets of simulations. They are not reenactments from a fixed script. They encourage students to read beyond the spoon-feeding to strengthen their case. Good ones require students to think about why things turned out as they did in actual fact—why the facts turned out the way they did.

Pace's second point deserves citation, "there is a nagging concern as to whether we can assume that all students have the cognitive abilities needed to conduct the complex mental operations required for embodying historical figures."[40] Put bluntly, are some students too dumb to be players in historical simulations?

This question raises others. Exactly what cognitive abilities are needed for those operations? One must be the ability to be human: to face issues and make decisions. Do I march with the workers or the suffragettes? Do I side with Galileo or the church? How do I win the Chinese civil war? Do I cross the street when the light is red or green?

This last is a joker, or is it? All the questions require processing information and applying that information to a decision. When to cross the street is rather binary, though even it requires other considerations: is the street deserted and narrow, or is it a six-lane freeway buzzing with traffic? Most humans have the cognitive abilities to take these factors into account before stepping off the curb.

Perhaps Pace was actually questioning the abilities of some students to take the multitude of historical factors—the context of those figures to be embodied—into account. It is true that doing so requires considerably more brainpower than looking at traffic lights. But the problem is that either the student is not getting, or does not know how to get, the necessary information to provide that context, or the student has the information but is overwhelmed by it.

The former should come as no surprise to critics of traditional teaching methods. Students receive "the facts" from a textbook or lecture, with an eye to the next quiz or test. Putting those facts to active, interpretive use is unknown to them. The latter has the same source. Even those students who can get information on their own are not accustomed to employing it beyond generating a rote, often multiple-choice, answer. Pace's skepticism, and Caplan's kind of philistinism, may be depressing, but both raise good points, the foremost being: what are we supposed to be doing in the classroom?

Every teacher loves good students. They are bright, diligent, responsive yet respectful (models of Caplan's conformists). But our classes, to paraphrase Abraham Lincoln, are not made up of all excellent students all of the time. If our objective is to prove that our students know something and have the high test scores to verify that, we obviously want those excellent students, just as a youth sports coach—for whom winning is the only thing—will play his or her best athletes all the time and let the other poor souls languish on the bench.[41] On the other hand, if we want to develop learning skills in all our students, we have to set Pace's concern about their cognitive abilities at the center of things and work on improving those abilities for everyone.

Our business should be to help all students learn by giving them practice at confronting complex problems, figuring out what they need to know to address those problems, and what they need to do to find that knowledge. Simulations are good at posing such problems. Consider those difficulties faced by a student-Churchill at the commencement of *Rivalries*. She or he, almost always, begins my semester and simulation confident of assuming the prime minister position within a week or so. How swiftly their hopes are dashed as they start learning about the realities of Great Britain in 1936. If you want to learn how to swim, get into the pool.

Can You as *Teacher* Beat Churchill?

Getting your students to see those underlying realities—Britain in 1936, Washington in 1789, Harrison in 1892—is your challenge. Winston Churchill enjoyed a remarkable career as a politician, statesman, and author. His speeches and writings sing. Who can forget his "we shall never surrender" address? His decisions look wise even in retrospect: his warnings about the menace of Nazism, his determination to fight on when Britain was alone, his concerns about Stalin and the growing power of the Soviet Union. But his very success as an author has played into the model of teaching that straitjackets much of what we do today. It blinds us to complexity, to the possibility of other outcomes. It contributes to our seeing history as a time line, destined to turn out the way it has. If we succeed in teaching our students to successfully memorize this time line, have we really taught them history? Have we imparted any skills that they will find useful, even necessary, after they graduate?

Citizenship

Caplan and others might argue we have not. Vanishingly few of our students will ever get jobs as historians. So what possible use could teaching them history have?

There are two broad replies. One argues that—teaching content aside—the way students learn history imparts skills useful, even necessary, in any career they might pursue. These skills include communication, the ability to build and work with teams, recognizing the connections in complex problems, and so on.

Another reply maintains that teaching content itself is valuable and indispensable. Its advocates are particularly strong in the United States, and their attention centers on the teaching of US history. The core of their case is that a democracy requires an informed and intelligent citizenry and, whether teaching history imparts intelligence or not, it certainly informs young US students of where their form of government and political society came from and why they should participate in it. There is a universal value in teaching history, and there are nearly universal requirements in any US school that students learn it.[42] School should produce not just good workers, but good citizens.

These broad replies are two halves of the same walnut. The same skills, and ways of imparting them, that make for good citizens also make for productive workers. Not just communication or team building, effective history teaching will also promote empathy, civic responsibility, and a sense of community.

This combination of learning objectives, and the use of active learning to reach them, is hardly novel. It resides at the core philosophy of progressive educator John Dewey, whose words of a century ago still seem apt:

> That the situation should be of such a nature as to arouse thinking means of course that it should suggest something to do which is not either routine or capricious—something, in other words, presenting what is new (and hence uncertain or problematic) and yet sufficiently connected with existing habits to call out an effective response. An effective response means one which accomplishes a perceptible result, in distinction from a purely haphazard activity, where the consequences cannot be mentally connected with what is done. The most significant question which can be asked, accordingly, about any situation or experience proposed to induce learning is what quality of problem it involves.[43]

Dewey was not writing about using simulations to induce such learning, but he might as well have been. Simulations not only encourage the students to learn history and skills useful in their future jobs, they also lead them into a set of areas that make them better citizens.

Empathy

Should history instruction teach empathy? The real question is: how can it not? I begin my course on the history of the Second World War with an extended lecture on the mind of Adolf Hitler. I think it is essential for my students to understand how he saw his world, why that vision drove him to seek power, and how it told him what to do with that power once he obtained it. They have to feel his fury at Germany's defeat in 1918, his conviction that Germany was the victim of a conspiracy of many enemies, and at the bottom of that conspiracy was a cabal of Jews, themselves not truly human, who plotted the downfall of the German race through a whole host of sinister means. To truly understand the origins of the Second World War in Europe, in other words, my students need to empathize with Hitler.

Needless to say, the student in *Great Power Rivalries* who represents Hitler must empathize with particular skill and in particular depth. The same applies to every student in my simulation. They have to step into the minds of their characters.

But that is not all they have to do, not if they want to advance their characters' goals within the simulation. The better they know the characters whom other students represent, the more ably they can meet their own goals. Students on teams of democratic nations in *Rivalries* usually discover this need-to-know more quickly. A Franklin Roosevelt who understands a Richard Russell will defer pressing civil rights measures until late in the semester, if at all, to get Russell's support in other regards. An Édouard Daladier will look for some common ground to ensure that a Léon Blum allies with him and not the French communists. Hitlers and Stalins, at least the more successful ones, realize that building teams gives better results than giving orders, and team building stems from understanding the goals and desires of prospective team members. For Hitler, Himmler or Hess might be easy to empathize with. Optimally, though, a Hitler would want to see Schacht's reservations about fiscal indiscipline or appearing like a bunch of crude thugs to the rest of the world. Or von Manstein's opposition to engaging in risky wars or devoting resources to Himmler's SS.

Why stop with just your national teammates? A really good Hitler would know about and play on conservatives' fear of communism. British Tories, and for that matter King Edward VIII, had little love for Reds. The French Right had an active fear of them, as did many US Republicans,[44] China's Jiang, and practically every living Japanese leader. It is not difficult to imagine a student-Hitler with excellent empathy able to marshal an anti-communist crusade during the years simulated in *Rivalries*.

Arguing this point might sound off-base, or even creepy. Empathy is a social skill usually associated with socially beneficial things. We want our caregivers and therapists and, hopefully, teachers to empathize with us. We want to be comfortable around other people. Usually that means seeking the company of people who are like us, or at least can easily empathize with us. Especially when wider environments seem divisive, hostile, or even threatening, an empathetic enclave seems especially inviting. It is hardly surprising that, in the middle of the presidency of Donald Trump, enrollments are rising at single-sex and historically Black colleges and universities, for example.[45]

Yet, as with all things human, empathy has its darker side. Empathy can cause hatred. Skilled empaths can stir hatred. Sympathy for the victims of ISIS's brutal, callous, and self-publicized attacks and executions led to widespread support among the publics of the West for strong military action and, in the case of fellow citizens who had joined ISIS, stripping of their citizenship rights. Hitler's ability to fan anti-Semitic passions helped lead to the Holocaust.[46]

Even so, the best remedy for the human divisions enhanced by empathy is to encourage more empathy among humans.[47] It may be hard, even repulsive, to get inside the head of an ISIS soldier or supporter. But doing so is as important for understanding the modern Middle East as empathy for the Nazis is in grasping why the Europe of eighty years ago was as it was. I use such a parallel deliberately, because no discipline is better equipped to teach the importance of empathy as a path to understanding than history. This is not to argue the trite trope of learning the lessons of the past by making dubious use of such parallels. Already commentators on the Middle East have seized upon the badly flawed metaphor of a new Thirty Years' War to explain current events in that region.[48]

History is well suited to teach empathy not only because it must; it is well suited because it can. It may be hard, even repulsive, to get inside the head of a Nazi leader or supporter. But doing so is considerably easier when that leader or supporter does not speak only from the grave.[49] There is some distance, the simulation as a buffer, to reduce the unease of such an encounter.

A historical simulation maintains this sort of distance, a kind of mask, inasmuch as its students are only representatives of their roles. Yet in compelling them to play those roles, it compels all students in the simulation to confront the outlooks, ideologies, and goals of the various characters in the simulation. When you step into a *Rivalries* classroom, you are going to have to deal with Nazis, fascists, communists, and imperialists, like it or not. You are going to learn how to deal with people who see the world differently than you do, and who might have far more or far less power in the world than you do. To survive and flourish, you are going to have to learn empathy. In the words of my most successful student-Hitler: "In the process of trying to win the Simulation, I learned in a highly personal way the goals, beliefs, passions, and limitations of a large cadre of important figures and governments, which I remember precisely even more than ten years later."[50]

Play and Civic Responsibility

Maybe all men are created equal, but they don't stay that way, and then there are the women too. Jeffersonian ideals aside, the stark fact is that most of our educational institutions today are dedicated to sifting through individuals and dividing them by ability, wealth, and background, among other things. Grammar schools had different reading groups.[51] Middle and high schools their sections or tracks. The most brutal segregation came in the college selection process and results, with those attending highly selective private institutions destined to lead those from poorer or public universities who, in turn, were minor lords over the community college grads and those of the lowest caste, the great unwashed without any degree. It should hardly be surprising that one of the most significant indicators of political preference, and ways of viewing society and oneself, now is the amount and type of education someone has.[52] Only rarely do students from different groups mingle with each other on anything approaching an equal basis—with one major exception: playtime.

Unstructured, unplanned play among students of differing interests
and abilities has become an increasingly rare phenomenon in our society.
The effects of this rarity have become increasingly apparent to teachers,
other professional educators, and parents recently. After moving to a new
school district in Connecticut with a much shorter recess period than the
old one in California, one mother noticed that her children were more
restless after school, struggled with homework, and had trouble getting
along with others. Educators in Arizona persuaded the state legislature to
mandate two recess periods per day. Disciplinary actions went down. Test
scores went up. Students' health improved.[53]

What is going on here? Dr. Robert Bilder, a neuropsychologist, credits
fostering creativity. "What is valuable for children is freedom where they
are solving problems with no predictable answer. When it is open ended,
they retain the curiosity to learn more things."[54] Biopsychology professor
Peter Gray has taken this argument much further. Over the past half century, he argues, the US educational system has seen a steady and significant
decline in time allowed for free play, and an equally steady and significant
rise in formal testing for specifically defined skills that has resulted in co-
lossal homework demands that further reduce free play for children and
stultifying teaching to the test while they are in school. Adult-organized
(and highly tiered) youth sports are highly valued (especially by ambitious
or desperate parents seeking the end-of-the-rainbow "full ride" to college);
informal play with the neighbors' kids is seen as a waste of time.[55]

But it isn't a waste, not for children, not for human society at large.
Informal, free play is inherently asymmetrical. Older children play with
younger. The dexterous play with the clumsy, the speedsters with the slow-
pokes, the strong or gifted with the weak or slow. Yet play they do, because at some level they understand the asymmetry and devise ways to
adjust for it. Nobody insisted on footraces all the time because they knew
it wasn't fun for some of the others. Maybe it was time for a puzzle game
of some sort. Nobody liked being picked last on a team of softball or tag
football, but the pitcher would refrain from the hard stuff toward the bottom of the order, or a would-be tagger would stumble or fall down at a
strategic moment to let the little kid score.

Such idyllic scenes were not everyday occurrences, to be sure. But far
more often than not, these play groups made their adjustments and shifts

to avoid their own destruction as one member or another would take their toys—and themselves—and depart. These informal, free play groups, in other words, taught their members a sort of civic responsibility. They created their own communities, something Dewey found lacking in classrooms a century ago, something still lacking today.

> Upon the playground, in game and sport, social organization takes place spontaneously and inevitably. There is something to do, some activity to be carried on, requiring natural divisions of labor, selection of leaders and followers, mutual cooperation and emulation. In the schoolroom the motive and the cement of social organization are alike wanting. Upon the ethical side, the tragic weakness of the present school is that it endeavors to prepare future members of the social order in a medium in which the conditions of the social spirit are eminently wanting.[56]

They did so by also teaching a sort of empathy. Too many footraces? You could see Tommy's look of dejection and discouragement as he slow-stepped over the finish line in a visible display of both. Time for something else, something he might find enjoyable.

Procrustean Education

As Dewey argued, good education should promote a sense of community. Whatever benefits formal education brings in US society, however, the ability of groups to adjust themselves to their members is not one of them. Instead, individuals are adjusted to their groups, just as Procrustes' victims were adjusted to his bed. Take a test and be assigned to the Robins or the Dodos, section A or section G, the Ivy League or the various trenches. Even when those tests indicate potentially great benefits in breaking the mold, the system bucks hard against it.

Consider the case of skipping grades. Or rather one case, a small sample to be sure but an illustrative one. Heather Rains skipped from kindergarten to second grade. Her test scores and academic skills were not in dispute. As she put it herself, "I thrived with more challenging work and wanted more."[57] She did thrive, academically, but found it difficult to establish friendships with her older classmates. While it is possible that there would have been difficulties in any case, the school's decision to force her to take recess with her age group, not her classmates, almost certainly failed to help the situation.

Heather was, and remains, the rare exception. Despite testing that shows that significant numbers of students could benefit from grade skipping, under 1 percent do. Schools don't like it. Neither do most parents, for the sincere but jaw-dropping reason that skipping might inhibit their child's social development because they would be associating (or playing) with children of a different age! Teachers fear that such skipping will only accelerate academic competition and make an already stressful classroom situation worse.[58] As for holding students back a grade, let's just say that Procrustes would be very proud of us.

Perhaps unwittingly, though, the school system does promote development of community in one of its classes: recess. On the court or in the playground, students are free to form their own associations and spend time as they like. They usually have fun. They usually play games. They have fun because they play freely.

The Challenges of Free Play: "Recess" in High School and College

Colleges, and most high schools,[59] do not have recess. They do not take groups of students, throw them together for a fixed period, and ask them to get to know each other and amuse themselves. They do not have free play. They do, of course, throw groups of students together in classrooms for a fixed period, but there is rarely anything resembling making acquaintance, amusement, or play. Usually, those classrooms are scenes of rather procrustean efforts. Everybody reads the same thing. Everybody listens to the same lectures. Everybody memorizes the same facts or formulas. Everybody takes the same tests and forgets most of the readings, lectures, facts, and formulas on their way out of the final exam. Another way is possible.

As earlier chapters here should demonstrate, there is a small but growing community of high school and college teachers who have discovered and employed classroom simulations to teach. But they are by no means alone.

Playing historical simulations in your classes will not bring about world peace. It won't even solve most of the problems with contemporary educational systems raised in this chapter. But it will offer students something they have precious little of, something they will take to naturally, and something that will teach them valuable skills useful well beyond the classroom. How to manage limited resources. How to manage those resources in groups with different ideas about that management. How to make informed decisions based on less-than-complete information. Some of us would be happy with just: how to make decisions.

All my colleagues concede that students in my *Great Power Rivalries* are highly enthusiastic, even excited, about the simulation. But some question whether any learning takes place. How can it, when there are no lectures, no formal discussion sessions and, above all, no tests and no teaching? Especially without tests, how can learning ever be measured? How can we be sure students are being challenged? How can we know that they are actually learning?

Dump the Lesson Plans and Lectures? Ban the Tests?

The usual response to these questions is to test the students. Have the students learned empathy? Let's devise a test for that. Have they improved their team-building and cooperative skills? There must be an examination on those things somewhere, preferably multiple choice.

In fact, there are ways to assess student learning, but not through the usual scantron sheet or bluebook. The literature on assessment is large. It is often frustrating.[60] But some of it does offer concrete suggestions for how to figure out if your students are figuring anything out. Stanford University's website Teaching Commons[61] suggests three:

A. Assign your students a problem to solve. Ask them to write down what they were thinking about as they moved to solve it. Read the thinking-about; worry less about the solution.
B. Ask students to write simply about how they use their time, especially their study time. Here, the objective is not to grade success or failure, but lead students into reflecting on their own study habits.

C. End class a few minutes early. Ask students to summarize the main points covered, and to ask any questions they have of the material. Again, the focus is not on getting the right answer, but seeing what was or was not learned.

These are all good ideas and I have no quarrel with them. Why should I? When your students participate in a simulation, they are, consciously or not, doing all three. In a simulation, they are not looking for the right answer. They are trying to solve problems, whether they are those fourth graders seeking world peace, high schoolers wrestling with workers and suffragists, or college students trying to survive the 1930s and 1940s. If, as an instructor, you can challenge your students to learn in this way, rather than read a text and spit it back to you, you really will beat Churchill.

Appendix

Finding Historical Simulations

Below is a list, hardly exhaustive, of resources if you are looking for an off-the-shelf simulation or ideas about how to modify or create your own. It is primarily concentrated in the field of history, though a dedicated searcher should have little difficulty locating online possibilities in nearly any field.

http://reactingconsortiumlibrary.org/
https://www.historysimulation.com/
https://teachinghistory.org/teaching-materials/ask-a-master-teacher/23691
https://www.socialstudiescentral.com/instructional-resources/interactive-simulations/
http://www.tccle.org/uploads/7/8/4/2/7842881/socialstudies-simulations
    forsharing.pdf
https://woodrow.org/wp-content/uploads/2019/05/WW-American-History-Report.pdf

Notes

Introduction

1. "Games," Reacting to the Past, accessed August 27, 2020, https://reacting.barnard.edu/consortium.

1. From Game to Simulation

1. Ernest R. May, *The Making of the Monroe Doctrine* (Cambridge, MA: Belknap Press, 1975).

2. Ernest R. May, *Strange Victory: Hitler's Conquest of France* (New York: Hill and Wang, 2000), 5.

3. Mark Herman and Volko Ruhnke, *Fire in the Lake: Insurgency in Vietnam* (Hanford, CA: GMT Games, 2014).

4. The outstanding exception was *Diplomacy*, designed by Allan Calhamer in 1959. A highly abstract game set in Europe around 1914, but with players able to ally or backstab each other at will, *Diplomacy*'s mechanics were simple, so most playtime was consumed with negotiating deals and, often, breaking them. Calhamer self-published the game, then titled *Realpolitik*, in 1958. It was professionally published as *Diplomacy* (Boston: Games Research, 1961).

5. An added disincentive to preparing classroom simulations is the still-widespread view of them as frivolous. When I, as an assistant professor, published *Fire When Ready* (Austin, TX: Metagaming Concepts, 1982), a simulation of predreadnought naval battles, my chair

was horrified that I listed it on my curriculum vitae. If I had to include it at all, he insisted, it should be as a "nonacademic" publication.

6. Mary Jane Treacy, *Greenwich Village, 1913: Suffrage, Labor, and the New Woman* (New York: Norton, 2015).

7. Eric S. Mallin and Paul V. Sullivan, *Stages of Power: Marlowe and Shakespeare, 1592* (Distributed by University of North Carolina Press, 2016).

8. Frederick Purnell Jr., Michael S. Pettersen, and Mark C. Carnes, *The Trial of Galileo: Aristotelianism, the "New Cosmology," and the Catholic Church, 1616–1633* (New York: Pearson Education, 2008).

2. Roles

1. "Instructor Resources," Reacting to the Past, accessed August 27, 2020, https://reacting.barnard.edu/.

2. These considerations regarding class size and numbers of roles are also discussed in chapter 5.

3. Nicolas W. Proctor and Margaret Storey, *Kentucky, 1861: Loyalty, State, and Nation* (New York: Norton, 2017).

4. Mark Higbee and James Brewer Stewart, *Frederick Douglass, Slavery, and the Constitution, 1845* (New York: Norton, 2019).

5. Nicolas Proctor, *Reacting to the Past Game Designer's Handbook* (Scott's Valley, CA: CreateSpace, 2018), 133–34.

6. Gregory Sarafin, student in *Great Power Rivalries*, fall 2013. Letter to author.

7. The student subsequently suspected that I had assigned "neutral" as a challenge or goad. Could be.

8. Except, apparently, the student assigned to represent Minnesota senator Eugene McCarthy, who deserted his antiwar position, and street followers, to support Democratic presidential nominee Hubert Humphrey. Conversation with Seth Offenbach, December 2018.

9. She became a high school teacher and has tried her hand at her own classroom simulations.

10. No simulation student ever managed to replicate Churchill's historical accomplishments, though some managed the equivalent, usually because in their cases France did not fall, the Soviets conquered Germany swiftly, or Germany imploded due to other factors. These factors are discussed in more detail in chapter 9.

11. Contact me at Michael.barnhart@stonybrook.edu.

12. These reminders are sometimes important. I have had student-Hitlers who insisted on devoting all resources to the German military for territorial conquest and refused to consider even mild (but expensive) anti-Jewish policies—not very Nazi-like.

13. See especially comments to the article "The Unpleasant Truth about the 1941 Parachuting of Rudolf Hess in England, Part 1," ZeroHedge, August 18, 2018, https://www.zerohedge.com/news/2018-08-17/unpleasant-truth-about-1941-parachuting-rudolf-hess-england-part-1.

14. Hitler's solution to this crisis—to label Hess insane—was hardly ideal, as it led many Germans to wonder how Hitler could have tolerated a madman in power next to him for so many years. Ian Kershaw, *Hitler: 1936–1945 Nemesis* (New York: Norton, 2001), 369–74.

15. And the last: Hess hanged himself in 1987 at age 93, the last inmate of Spandau prison.

16. I also assign the Hess character control of the German navy. Why? Primarily because otherwise no one on the German team will care about naval affairs, to the immense relief of the British. Someone needs to be an advocate for spending on battleships or submarines. It cannot be von Manstein or Himmler. They each have their own armed forces to lobby for.

Schacht would be a stretch, and an impossibility if the student morphs into Goebbels. So, Hess gets the navy's portfolio for the sake of team dynamics.

17. See chapter 5 for a consideration of the physical environment of classroom simulations.

18. I do have the students on the US team run the presidential contest of 1936, but as a training exercise. A Republican victory was historically not in the cards.

19. Here I give Chinese proper names first romanized under the Pinyin method, second using the older Wade-Giles style.

20. Not just students, as the tremendous popularity of cosplaying attests.

21. For the students on the Japan team, I try to deepen the atmosphere by lending actual *hanko* for them to use in lieu of their signatures on their turnsheets.

22. The two exceptions: (a) one student-Hitler wore a Wehrmacht uniform, without signs of rank or specialty and without armband, to the last day of class. He had established himself during the semester as an odd duck and the other students offered no reaction besides the usual eye-rolls; (b) a student-Himmler hosted an off-campus party for her teammates which, I was later informed, had red, black, and white banners and hand-drawn SS bolts displayed. The teammates reported the details to me, but as the event was off-campus and by invitation, I had no authority to act. In any case, the reporting students were more amused than appalled.

23. As explained in chapter 5.

24. Usually in these cases the student-Hitler will follow reality and announce her or his Hitler as having committed suicide before any trial.

25. More successful German teams usually devote considerable effort early in the simulation to proving to France and Britain that the communists are a much graver threat to the West than Nazism.

26. Judith Shapiro, "Fragile Students, Fragile Democracy?" (keynote speech, Nineteenth Annual Faculty Institute: Democratic Education in Uncertain Times, Reacting to the Past Institute, Barnard College, June 14, 2019).

27. Robert Goodrich, "Democracy in Crisis" gamebook, unpublished draft 1.3, summer 2019, 1–2. Used with permission.

28. A case in point is the reproduction of George Grosz, *The Pillars of Society* (1926, oil on canvas, 200 x 108 cm, Berlin, Nationalgalerie, Staatliche Museen zu Berlin) that appears on the front cover of Goodrich's gamebook. Grosz may have intended an intellectual point, but the image goes straight for the gut.

29. In the summer of 2019, one candidate for the Mississippi state senate used video footage of himself assaulting a journalist and bragging that doing so made him a better candidate for office.

30. Avoiding emotional subjects can be harder than you think. See Carnes' discussion of the impact on one student of *Josianic Reform: Deuteronomy, Prophecy, and the Israelite Religion* set in the supposedly distant year of 622 BCE. Mark C. Carnes, *Minds on Fire: How Role-Immersion Games Transform College* (Cambridge, MA: Harvard University Press, 2014), 115–19.

31. It is also prudent, whether the simulation is the course or any part of the course, to clearly note on the course syllabus what the simulation involves and under what conditions a student may participate or opt out.

3. Rules

1. This mechanic is not historically accurate. It is designed to limit snowballing majorities, on the one hand, and give students who are at the bottom of the totem pole some help in climbing back up.

2. For aspiring Churchills, the British constituencies are similar, with Workers replacing Sans-culottes and Pensioners replacing Artisans.

3. As recent studies have shown, the Chinese communists' first efforts at such conversion were disastrous. Mao did learn from them, and an especially able student-Mao will ferret out these efforts and perhaps even argue that they should be given a second chance if their first conversion fails. See Yang Kuisong, "Nationalist and Communist Guerrilla Warfare in North China," in *The Battle for China: Essays on the Military History of the Sino-Japanese War of 1937–1945*, ed. Mark Peattie, Edward Drea, and Hans van de Ven (Stanford, CA: Stanford University Press, 2011), chap. 12.

4. Available upon request.

4. Requirements

1. Letter to author from Abigail duFour (Hitler in *Rivalries*, fall 2005).

2. Cathy Davidson, in her *The New Education: How to Revolutionize the University to Prepare Students for a World in Flux* (New York: Basic Books, 2017), points to a series of studies illustrating this point. Students were divided into three sets. One received just letter grades on their assignments. One received only comments, without grades. The third received both comments and grades. The group showing the most improvement over time was the second—no grades—not the third. Davidson, 195–97.

3. Of course the anonymous student author is known to the instructor, just not the other students.

4. Names disguised.

5. Room

1. Nicolas Proctor, *Forest Diplomacy: Cultures in Conflict on the Pennsylvania Frontier, 1757* (New York: Norton, 2018); Jace Weaver and Laura Adams Weaver, *Red Clay, 1835: Cherokee Removal and the Meaning of Sovereignty* (New York: Norton, 2017); Ainslie Embree and Mark Carnes, *Defining a Nation: India on the Eve of Independence, 1945* (New York: Norton, 2016).

2. Except Jiang Jieshi, who is barely head of what is barely a state in 1936.

3. There are rare exceptions. See chapter 7.

4. With a very large class, historical ambassadors could have roles, though these would become awkward if their nation went to war with their host.

5. See Reacting to the Past Consortium, Big List of Reacting Games, available through the Reacting website: "Instructor Resources," Reacting to the Past, accessed August 28, 2020, https://reacting.barnard.edu/.

6. Nicolas Proctor, *Chicago, 1968* (copyright under Reacting Consortium, 2018), "Games: Games under Review," Reacting to the Past, accessed August 28, 2020, https://reacting.barnard.edu/.

7. See for example the survey run by Nicolas Proctor on student interaction in his simulations. Nicolas Proctor, *Reacting to the Past Game Designer's Handbook* (Scott's Valley, CA: CreateSpace, 2018), 121.

6. The A.I.

1. Frederick Purnell Jr., Michael S. Pettersen, and Mark C. Carnes, *The Trial of Galileo: Aristotelianism, the "New Cosmology," and the Catholic Church, 1616–1633* (New York: Pearson Education, 2008), 37.

2. Usually, however, I will kill off Neville Chamberlain sometime in late 1940 (he actually died in November of that year). It is a kludge that I am not fond of, but unless the student playing Chamberlain is incompetent or fantastically unfortunate in British elections, she or he can build a faction impervious to no-confidence votes, stay in power regardless of the situation elsewhere in Europe, and prompt bitter student rebellions, especially from the student representing Churchill. As it is, student-Chamberlains will accept their character's death with grace, or at least resignation.

3. Clay lost by only 40,000 votes nationally.

4. Which of course it does, in binary notation.

5. Amazon's airing of *The Man in the High Castle*, a tale set in a world in which Nazi Germany and Imperial Japan conquer the world and divide the United States between them, has opened some minds. Alas, few students seeing it have bothered to read the original novel by Philip Dick, which has a message not illuminated in the screen version.

6. In this instance, the student-Himmler calculated that he would have most effect by convincing the students on the British and French teams that they were failing to act in-character by appeasing the Soviet Union over the Red regime in Germany. After considerable persistence, he succeeded, and made the simulation much more interesting for everyone than if he had just entered the glowering corner.

7. The chief student complaint about my colleague Eric Zolov's first run of his *Cuba in the Cold War* simulation was exactly on this point. His students at times were not sure what was possible and what was not.

8. Josiah Ober, Naomi Norman, and Mark Carnes, *The Threshold of Democracy: Athens in 403 BCE*, 4th ed. (New York: Norton, 2015).

9. There is an impressive story of just such role-playing success in Mark C. Carnes, *Minds on Fire: How Role-Immersion Games Transform College* (Cambridge, MA: Harvard University Press, 2018), 128–30.

10. Actually, I use an online random number generator that itself has a random seed, and I make sure the students know that I do. No loaded dice! See "Random Integer Generator," Random.Org, accessed August 28, 2020, https://www.random.org/.

11. Carnes, *Minds on Fire*, 115–18.

7. Under the Hood

1. A copy of *The Daily Planet* that I did write from students' turnsheets appears in chapter 6.

2. The details of the seed and process can be found at: "Random Integer Generator," Random.Org, accessed August 28, 2020, https://www.random.org/.

3. There is no deficit spending in *Great Power Rivalries*.

4. Files listing these Policy Options are available from the author.

5. Waldo Heinrichs argues that Roosevelt approved the freeze to prevent an attack on the Soviet Union in his persuasive *Threshold of War* (New York: Oxford University Press, 1988).

8. Simulations for an Afternoon

1. One possibility is Marshall Hayes and Eric Nelson, *London 1854: Cesspits, Cholera, and Conflict over the Broad Street Pump*, a simulation of the cholera epidemic in 1854. Available to instructors from http://reactingconsortiumlibrary.org.

2. The Reacting Consortium also currently has a nearly completed simulation of its own on the Missile Crisis by Ray Kimball and Kimberly Redding. See Kimball and Redding,

Eyeball to Eyeball: The Cuban Missile Crisis Simulation, available from http://reactingcon sortiumlibrary.org. John Moser of the Consortium has his own, lengthier, simulations of 1914 Europe and Japan in 1940–41. See Moser, *Europe on the Brink, 1914: The July Crisis* (Chapel Hill: University of North Carolina Press, 2020); Moser, *Japan, Pan-Asianism, and the West, 1940–41*, available from http://reactingconsortiumlibrary.org.

3. This need for reaching a swift friction point is one reason why *Greenwich Village*, *Galileo*, and *Stages*, among others, customarily have a decisive class session—a march, a trial, or a Privy Council decision—that arrives fairly quickly to bring the simulation to an end.

4. Laurence Chang and Peter Kornbluh, eds., *The Cuban Missile Crisis, 1962: A National Security Archive Documents Reader* (New York: New Press, 1999).

5. To be published by Norton in 2020, materials available for download through the Reacting Consortium website, http://reactingconsortiumlibrary.org. Used with permission.

6. Ultimately, the instructor will end the impasse by introducing a foreign variable, usually from either the United States or Soviet Union. It's best to let student frustration mount for a while, to drive home this central teaching point.

7. In this particular case, judicious choice of selections directly from Tuchman can serve as functional equivalents to role sheets, with the potential bonus of enticing students to read other parts of her book. Barbara W. Tuchman, *The Guns of August, August 1914* (London: New English Library, 1964).

8. Future sessions made sure that all teams were on the same floor. Physical layouts matter!

9. As a first step, you could use these guidelines to modify an existing simulation for your particular needs.

10. Hayes and Nelson, *London 1854*.

11. With acknowledgement to Orson Scott Card's science fiction tale, *Speaker for the Dead* (London: Arrow, 1986).

12. Ursula LeGuin, *Always Coming Home* (London: Gollancz, 1986).

9. Can You Beat Churchill?

1. William Manchester, *The Last Lion: Winston Spencer Churchill; Alone, 1932–1940* (Boston: Little, Brown, 1983), 188, quoting Harold Nicolson. Manchester's study is magisterial, but a classic case of reading historical events through hindsight.

2. Giving Germany such an option, rather than forcing an abdication crisis on Britain, is in keeping with my design philosophy of granting maximum possible flexibility to students, much as I allow Italy to decide when, or whether, to trigger civil wars in Spain, Yugoslavia, or Greece. Edward's well-known trip to Germany after abdication also gives some flavor to allowing the Nazis when, or whether, to turn him in the simulation's world.

3. Churchill's initial appointment had been minister without portfolio.

4. When they were not thwarted altogether by British cabinet inclinations to send forces elsewhere, such as the politically significant port of Trondheim.

5. And even prewar, for the United States, as in the Atlantic Charter of August 1941.

6. Churchill's journey in writing these volumes is expertly traced by David Reynolds, *In Command of History* (New York: Random House, 2005).

7. A thoughtful exposition of this influence appears in Ernest May, *"Lessons" of the Past: The Use and Misuse of History in American Foreign Policy* (Oxford: Oxford University Press, 1973), chaps. 2–3.

8. Bruce Lesh, *"Why Won't You Just Tell Us the Answer?" Teaching Historical Thinking in Grades 7–12* (Portland, ME: Stenhouse, 2011).

9. Robert Barr and John Tagg, "From Teaching to Learning—a New Paradigm for Undergraduate Education," *Change* 27, no. 6 (November/December 1995): 13–25.

10. Barr and Tagg, 24.

11. Bryan Caplan, *The Case against Education: Why the Education System Is a Waste of Time and Money* (Princeton: Princeton University Press, 2018).

12. Though not very effectively, it seems. Only half of US adults can work out that saving five cents a gallon on 140 gallons of oil comes out to seven dollars. Caplan, chap. 2.

13. For a spirited defense of such completion rates, see "Stop Asking about Completion Rates: Better Questions to Ask about MOOCs in 2019," EdSurge, November 28, 2018, https://www.edsurge.com/news/2018-11-28-stop-asking-about-completion-rates-better-questions-to-ask-about-moocs-in-2019.

14. Michael Eisenberg and Gerhard Fischer, "MOOCs: A Perspective from the Learning Sciences," in *Learning and Becoming in Practice: 11th International Conference of the Learning Sciences (ICLS), 2014*, ed. J. L. Polman et al. (Boulder, CO: International Society of the Learning Sciences, 2014), 190–97; article also online at http://l3d.cs.colorado.edu/~gerhard/papers/2014/ICLS-MOOCS.pdf.

15. The COVID-19 pandemic of 2020 highlighted the radical disparities in resources and outcomes of online learning. Dana Goldstein, "2 Schools, Private and Public, Illustrate the Gap in Remote Learning," *New York Times*, May 10, 2020, 23.

16. Using in-person student groups to learn, but with modular access to online resources, is at the center of Michael Horn and Heather Staker's *Blended: Using Disruptive Innovation to Improve Schools* (San Francisco: Jossey-Bass, 2015).

17. Eliza Gray, "Are Liberal Arts Colleges Doomed? The Cautionary Tale of Hampshire College and the Broken Business Model of American Higher Education," *Washington Post Magazine*, October 21, 2019, https://www.washingtonpost.com/magazine/2019/10/21/downfall-hampshire-college-broken-business-model-american-higher-education/?arc404=true.

18. David Parlett, *The Oxford History of Board Games* (Oxford: Oxford University Press, 1999), chap. 4.

19. *The Oregon Trail* dates to 1971 and was written on an early version of BASIC explicitly for classroom use. It became a commercial success by the late 1980s.

20. That is, a machine being able to exhibit human responses and behavior.

21. "Teaching with Simulations," Harvard Business Publishing: Education, accessed August 31, 2020, https://hbsp.harvard.edu/simulations-feature/. See also Jonathan Moules, "Business Schools Embrace Games as a Learning Tool," *Financial Times*, December 2, 2019, 15.

22. Roger Kneebone et al., "Distributed Simulation—Accessible Immersive Training," *Medical Teacher* 32, no. 1 (January 2010): 65–70.

23. James Lacey, "Wargaming in the Classroom: An Odyssey," War on the Rocks, April 19, 2016, https://warontherocks.com/2016/04/wargaming-in-the-classroom-an-odyssey/.

24. Lacey, "Wargaming in the Classroom."

25. Christopher S. Stowe, Bradford A. Wineman, and Paul D. Gelpi, "Staff Riding in the Twenty-First Century: A Need for Pedagogical Change?," *Army History* 110 (Winter 2019): 20–27.

26. It is odd that Caplan, in *The Case against Education*, does not consider the US military in his study, as it is one of the largest education providers to US students without college degrees or, for that matter, high school diplomas.

27. Damone Moore, quoted in "Warriors in the Civilian Workforce: Helping Veterans Transition," RAND Review, October 28, 2015, https://www.rand.org/blog/rand-review/2015/10/warriors-in-the-civilian-workforce.html.

28. Chaitra Hardison and Michael Shanley, "Essential Skills Veterans Gain during Professional Military Training," RAND Corporation, 2016, https://www.rand.org/pubs/tools/TL160z2-2.html.

29. For example, J. L. G. Ferris, *The First Thanksgiving 1621*, photomechanical print, Library of Congress Prints and Photographs Division, Lot 4579, accessed August 31, 2020, https://www.loc.gov/item/2001699850/.

30. Samuel Wineburg, *Why Learn History (When It's Already on Your Phone)* (Chicago: University of Chicago Press, 2018), 94.

31. Historians do well in critically evaluating context, authenticity, and reliability in historical documents, but do not seem to apply the same standards otherwise. For a withering and depressing consideration of this problem, see Caplan, *The Case against Education*, chap. 7.

32. For example, see Samuel Wineburg, Mark Smith, and Joel Breakstone, "What Is Learned in College History Classes?," *Journal of American History* 104 (March 2018): 983–93.

33. Wineburg, *Why Learn History*, chap. 6.

34. John Hunter, *World Peace and Other 4th-Grade Achievements* (New York: Houghton Mifflin, 2013).

35. And sometimes very predictable places. See Brittney Lewer, "Reimagining American History Education," Princeton: The Woodrow Wilson National Fellowship Foundation, May 2019, p. 9, https://woodrow.org/wp-content/uploads/2019/05/WW-American-History-Report.pdf.

36. A question I have gotten more than once in my classes.

37. Mark Bauerlein, *The Dumbest Generation: How the Digital Age Stupefies Young Americans and Jeopardizes Our Future* (New York: Penguin, 2008), chap. 2.

38. "Reviews of Role-Playing Classroom Games: Reacting to the Past," *American Historical Review* 125 (February 2020): 146–59.

39. The simulation Pace reviewed focused on art in transition in Paris, 1888–1889, but the parallels to such simulations as *Galileo* or *Stages* are clear.

40. "Reviews of Role-Playing Classroom Games," 154.

41. Trenchant points made by Jennifer Etnier, "Your Kids' Coach Is Probably Doing It Wrong," *New York Times*, March 11, 2020, https://www.nytimes.com/2020/03/11/opinion/youth-sports-coaches.html?te=1&nl=david-leonhardt&emc=edit_ty_20200311&campaign_id=39&instance_id=16651&segment_id=22081&user_id=91bfcc3f5282b89baae3adb3ddab2fe1&regi_id=5717747920200311.

42. Outside the United States, the teaching of citizenship can be different. See, for example, Wiel Veugelers and Isolde de Groot, "Theory and Practice of Citizenship Education," in *Education for Democratic Intercultural Citizenship*, ed. Wiel Veugelers (Leiden: Brill, 2019), 14–41.

43. John Dewey, *Democracy and Education* (New York: Macmillan, 1916), chap. 12.

44. And conservative Democrats, especially in the US South.

45. Alina Tugend, "When College Is Also a Haven," *New York Times*, February 24, 2019.

46. Paul Bloom, "The Dark Side of Empathy," *Atlantic*, September 25, 2015, https://www.theatlantic.com/science/archive/2015/09/the-violence-of-empathy/407155/.

47. Fritz Breithaupt strongly disagrees; see Fritz Breithaupt and Andrew Hamilton, *The Dark Sides of Empathy* (Ithaca, NY: Cornell University Press, 2019).

48. Lorenzo Kamel, "There Is No Thirty Years' War in the Middle East," The National Interest, August 29, 2016, https://nationalinterest.org/feature/there-no-thirty-years-war-the-middle-east-17513.

49. There are a few bold instructors, such as mine in Northwestern University's School of Speech, who in 1971 invited Frank Collin, head of the National Socialist Party of America, to address us students in a course on demagoguery. Mr. Collin was not informed of the name of the course. He and an escort arrived in full regalia and, amazingly, made it on and off campus without violence.

50. Letter to author from Abigail duFour (Hitler in *Rivalries*, fall 2005).

51. Children can be cruel and my grammar school classmates were no exception. The teacher assigned birds' names to our reading groups, "Robins," "Cardinals," or "Blue jays," but we always termed the slowest readers as belonging to the "Dodos."

52. These words were written before the college admissions cheating scandal of March 2019. The scandal, alas, only confirms them.

53. Laura Holson, "Running, Jumping and Swinging Their Way to a Lifetime of Innovation," *New York Times*, March 2, 2019.

54. Holson, "Running, Jumping and Swinging."

55. Peter Gray, *Free to Learn* (New York: Basic Books, 2013).

56. John Dewey, *The School and Society* (Chicago: University of Chicago Press, 1907), chap. 1.

57. Tim Walker, "Should More Students Be Allowed to Skip a Grade?," NEAToday, March 27, 2017, http://neatoday.org/2017/03/27/should-more-students-skip-a-grade/.

58. The same sort of debates, with slightly different variables, are common for children in organized youth or school sports. It is exceptionally rare for even the most gifted young athletes to be allowed to play above their age. Then there are parental concerns, often deep, over the cut-off birthdates for entering kindergarten.

59. A few high schools are experimenting with recess. "Unplugging From Stress," Edutopia, February 3, 2015, https://www.edutopia.org/practice/recess-high-school-students.

60. Wineburg's article in "Reviews of Role-Playing Classroom Games" concludes on the grim note that the history teacher had better figure out assessment procedures, since their supervisors were demanding them. "Reviews of Role-Playing Classroom Games," 125. Nearly as depressing is an otherwise insightful article by Chris Balow that resorts, ultimately, to testing. See Balow, "7 Methods for Measuring Student Growth, " Illuminate Education, December 14, 2017, https://www.illuminateed.com/blog/2017/12/7-methods-measuring-student-growth/.

61. "Assessing Student Learning," Stanford Teaching Commons, accessed April 13, 2020, https://teachingcommons.stanford.edu/resources/teaching/evaluating-students/assessing-student-learning (article removed from site as of August 31, 2020).

INDEX

Tōjō Hideki, 125–27
Treacy, Mary Jane, 18
Tresckow, Henning von, 37
*The Trial of Galileo: Aristotelianism,
the "New Cosmology," and the
Catholic Church, 1616–1633* (Purnell,
Pettersen, and Carnes): conflict in,
112; debriefing and reflection, 102–3;
ending, 101, 174n3(ch.8); evaluation
and grades, 73–74; instructor
responsibilities, 92–93; overview,
2, 19–20; roles, 21–22, 24–25, 89;
room factor, 80–81, 85; rules, 58, 88;
structure, 106; subject matter, 3, 72;
writing assignments, 74, 100
trials, 134–35
trigger-alerts, 29. *See also* sensitive
issues
Truman, Harry, 132
Trump, Donald, 160
Tuchman, Barbara, *The Guns of August,*
127–28, 174n7(ch.8)
turnsheets, 88, 93, 95, 106–9, 171n21

U-Boat (game), 6–9
uncertainties, 89–90, 130–31
unionists, 84. *See also Greenwich Village,
1913*
United Federation of Teachers (UFT),
132–33
United States: Cuban missile crisis,
119–23; elections, 64–66, 171n18;
Policy Options in *Great Power
Rivalries,* 47–49; roles in *Great
Power Rivalries,* 42–43, 46–49; rules
in *Rivalries,* 64–66; value of studying
history of, 158. *See also Great Power
Rivalries; Greenwich Village, 1913*

US military: educational methods,
149–51, 175n26; war-gaming models,
11
*US Response to the Ebola Outbreak,
2014–2015* (simulation), 23
USSR. *See* Soviet Union

victory conditions, 8–9, 56
video gamers, 154
Vietnam, 12–14
von Klüge, Gunther, 37–38
von Manstein, Erich, 35–38, 42, 60, 159,
170n16

Wang Jingwei (Wang Ching-wei), 49–50,
66–70, 76–77, 84, 90
war games. *See* games/war games
Washington, George, 153
West Germany, 11
Willkie, Wendell, 47–48, 64
Wilson, Woodrow, 57, 89
Wineburg, Sam, 152–54, 177n60
women's rights, 18, 58. See also
Greenwich Village, 1913
World Peace (Hunter), 154
World War I, 127–28
World War II: contingency and, 10–12;
political and social factors in, 12–13.
See also *Great Power Rivalries,
1936–1947;* Midway, 1942
writing assignments, 74, 100, 143.
See also journals, student

X, Malcolm, 133–34
Xi'an Incident (1936), 67, 70

Zhukov, Georgy, 77
Zolov, Eric, 173n7

CPSIA information can be obtained
at www.ICGtesting.com
Printed in the USA
LVHW030542010322
712297LV00002B/245